Praise for *G[...]*
What You C[...]

"We never know when we might find ourselves in dire
circumstances. This beautifully and sensitively written
book by Anita Agers-Brooks tells true stories of various
individuals who faced overwhelming circumstances and
discovered the victorious life Christ died to offer us.
Anita offers very specific steps you can take to climb out
of despair and find the real and certain hope that exists.
I highly recommend *Getting Through What You Can't
Get Over*, with its strong biblical principles that you can
depend on. Give a copy to a loved one who is suffering; it
will be a godsend."

–Pamela Christian—The Faith Doctor with
Your Rx for Life, author of *Examine Your Faith!
Finding Truth in a World of Lies* and *Renew
Your Hope! Remedy for Personal Breakthroughs*

"*Getting Through What You Can't Get Over* by Anita Agers-
Brooks offers help, hope, and healing insight. She rolls
back the rules on transparency in telling personal stories
and explores the process of returning to life anew. A must-
read for those caught in the grip of pain, as well as those
who desire to support someone who's struggling. This is an
amazing book and will help a lot of hurting people."

–Deb DeArmond, speaker, coach, cofounder of
WordGirls, and author of *I Choose You Today: 31 Choices
to Make Love Last* and *Related by Chance, Family by Choice*

"The first chapter gripped my heart and emotions. The stories are breathtaking, honest, and transparent. I wept through the first chapter and raced to start the next. Anita's willingness to address tough issues will touch the hearts of women all over the world. Far too often we hide, live in secrecy, and wear our shame. Anita gives practical and helpful tips on how to cope, come out of the darkness, and heal. *Getting Through What You Can't Get Over* will inspire and encourage women. They will come away understanding they are not alone in their suffering and see that freedom is possible."

–Tina Samples, Golden Scroll Award–winning author of *Wounded Women of the Bible: Finding Hope When Life Hurts*

"Anita shares from the deep painful places of her life and her walk with God. Through the power of her stories, we are given an intimate glimpse into the inner working of overcoming depression and times of brokenness. *Getting Through What You Can't Get Over* should be required reading for every person battling depression and for those who love them."

–Saundra Dalton-Smith, MD, physician, speaker, and author of *Set Free to Live Free*

"Anita uses true stories, powerful scriptures, and practical wisdom to take trembling hands and gently slip them into the healing hands of Jesus."

–Cheryl Ricker, author of *Rush of Heaven*

"I love the descriptive stories and easy-to-read style in *Getting Through What You Can't Get Over*. Instead of offering peachy, instant answers, Anita Brooks offers solid tips. The variety of suggestions, including healing songs and scriptures, gives realistic hope for people in terrible situations."

–Lucille Zimmerman, MA, licensed professional counselor and author of *Renewed: Finding Your Inner Happy in an Overwhelmed World*

"Anita Agers-Brooks has penned not only a book about recovery from emotional and spiritual pain but a book packed with practical advice, insights, and tools to help you do exactly what she promises in her title, *Getting Through What You Can't Get Over*. By sharing stories of the painful experiences we encounter, Anita also makes it clear that we all have to deal with some form of post-traumatic stress; none of us are immune to grieving, hurting, emotional, and psychological pain, and the sooner we learn to treat ourselves kindly as we suffer, the healthier we will be. Her Insider Insights at the end of each chapter are perfect 'cheat sheets' you can use to kick-start your day with music, scripture, and prayer. I have no doubt that I will refer to them often when my own inspiration runs low!"

–Jan Dunlap, author of *Saved by Gracie* and the *Birder Murder Mysteries*

"*Getting Through What You Can't Get Over* is a must-read for anyone who has personally experienced some sort of trauma in their lifetime or has encountered someone with post-traumatic stress disorder. Anita Agers-Brooks effectively conveys her own inner struggles, as well as those of many others, and encourages us all to live in the reality of God's grace, love, peace, and joy. Anita's 'Insider Insights' at the end of each chapter give guidance for emotional healing, practical help, spiritual comfort, and prayer. Even though your heart will ache as you read the stories in each chapter, you will definitely benefit from God's comfort offered in this book through His Holy Spirit."

–Debbie Moore, Women's Missions & Ministry Consultant, Arkansas Baptist State Convention

"*Getting Through What You Can't Get Over: Inspiration to Help You Move Past Your Pain into Lasting Freedom* is an encouraging and inspiring read, especially for someone who has experienced depression, anxiety, or PTSD."

–Dr. J. D. Stake, LPC LMFT-S

"Agers-Brooks dislikes people saying, 'Let go and let God.' She says she desperately wanted to let go, 'but how do you let go of things you can't get over?' That's a question many of us ask. We all face those terrible times when life just doesn't work right. She presents a broad area of personal issues, and each chapter closes with practical and spiritual insights to enable readers to move through their own heartaches."

–Cecil Murphey, author or co-author of more than 130 books including *90 Minutes in Heaven* with Don Piper and *Gifted Hands: The Ben Carson Story*.

ANITA AGERS-BROOKS

GETTING *Through* WHAT *Get Over*

Stories, Tips, and Inspiration

to Help You Move Past

Your Pain into Lasting Freedom

SHILOH RUN PRESS

An Imprint of Barbour Publishing, Inc.

Print ISBN 978-1-68322-950-6

eBook Editions:
Adobe Digital Edition (.epub) 978-1-63409-290-6
Kindle and MobiPocket Edition (.prc) 978-1-63409-291-3

Published by Shiloh Run Press, an imprint of Barbour Publishing, Inc., 1810 Barbour Drive, Uhrichsville, Ohio 44683, www.shilohrunpress.com

Our mission is to inspire the world with the life-changing message of the Bible.

Member of the
Evangelical Christian
Publishers Association

Printed in the United States of America.

DEDICATION

To those who are trying to get through something you will never get over, please know you are not alone. God sees you and loves what He sees. Also to Pam and Cheryl. God saved you by the valley, allowing you to walk in paradise with Jesus. May your legacy strengthen many to move forward, when their road-weary souls need courage to take one more step.

ACKNOWLEDGMENTS

Because of many, this book and others exist. There are things I'll never get over, but because of you, I made it through.

My deepest appreciation goes to my family for your love and patience. Madison, Ryan, Dakota, Mom, Dad, my siblings, Charlie and Jean, along with extended members. Ricky, you deserve an award, for without you, none of this would exist. I am so proud of the man God made, and your willingness to honor Him with your life. I am blessed that you are my faithful and awe-mazing husband.

Thank you into eternity and beyond to my friends. Mary, Jeana, Glenda, Sharon, Sandy, Laura, Ashley, Tera, Bear, Jess, Karen, Kathy, Lisa, Lucille, Edie, and others too many to name. Allison, I must thank you especially for listening to God, and allowing Him to use you so powerfully for such a time as this.

I'm grateful for my local and global church family, and my network of friends from many organizations and industries who added much-needed prayers, insights, and several atta gal's. CLC Rolla, FBC Steelville, CLASSeminars, Stonecroft Ministries, the super fun Paddlesports industry, Zenith Zone, LLC, SLU Hospital, the Steelville Arts Council, and many more. Of course, I must mention my favorite coffee shop, Art & Joe's in Steelville, MO.

To the entire team at Barbour Publishing, thank you for your excellence. I am humbled at how you transformed my words into a work of art.

Finally, I must offer my great respect and regard for those whose stories are represented in this book. Your courage, your wisdom, and your honesty will change lives and make a difference in the world. You matter, and I am honored to know you.

CONTENTS

INTRODUCTION

G od did not create us to be miserable. Yet there are
times we think we'll never laugh again. Maybe you
feel that way now.

None of us wants to learn from painful experiences,
but life doesn't always offer us a choice. We are
challenged early and often with plenty of adversity.
These are the kinds of things we don't get over, so how
in the world do we survive when life won't leave us in
peace?

Through this book, I want to explore the answer
to that question with you, offering emotional and
practical ideas that have helped others, professional
tips from those educated to serve recipients of trauma,
and spiritual wisdom offered by the One who sees your
hurts and cares about what He sees.

But I won't tell you simply to put on your happy face.
The New International Version translation of Proverbs
25:20 says, "Like one who takes away a garment on
a cold day, or like vinegar poured on a wound, is one
who sings songs to a heavy heart." My goal is to offer a
realistic yet hope-filled view of situations people endure.

In this book, I share real-life stories, some as
compilations based on true events from many people
who survived similar, yet difficult and excruciating
circumstances. I warn you, some will make you squirm.
But they will resonate with real life, real challenges, and
real victory.

In some cases, names and details are changed to protect the privacy and hearts of those who lived what you will read. For them, the words in this book are more than mere stories, the lessons more than a degree from the University of Unimaginable Pain. Their varied outcomes are more than a process of healing.

For these ordinary people, this represents their extraordinary lives—full of unwanted surprises. Some stem from traumas in the body, others from tragedies of the wallet, while all pierce the heart.

But the shock of their stories doesn't come from circumstance. It's in the hope that no matter what, one day pain-filled people may laugh yet again.

CHAPTER 1

Valley Walker

W hen I met her, I was in the blackest hole I'd ever
experienced. I cowered in a deep pit of depression and anxiety spawned by betrayal. The pain was raw
and unquenchable. Each day I tried to scale the walls
and scramble into some light, but with every attempt
I slid back down the slimy slopes of the well and
crumpled into the darkness of my despair.

My attendance at the conference was a miracle,
considering most days I barely had the strength to pull
myself from bed. Taking a shower required a great deal
of effort. But a friend had urged me to go with her, to
see the former Auschwitz prisoner of war and motivational speaker Dr. Edith Eger. Yet at the last minute,
my friend couldn't go. To this day, I can't explain how I
ended up there. Alone.

It was immediately evident that Edie was a force of
nature not to be denied. I first noticed her easy manner
as she made her way among the group dignitaries,
each marked by little square badges neatly pinned to
dresses and suits. Her movements spoke of someone
with courage, plunging into unknown arenas, finding
confidence because she dared.

When Edie took the stage, my heart fluttered.
Maybe it was her energy, a reminder of the absence of

my own. Maybe it was knowing she understood hellish pain, and in my desperation, hoping she would tell me how to smile again. Maybe it was God, giving me a glimpse of what was coming.

Her silver hair was groomed in a stylish yet practical mass of short curls. It accented the ever-changing emotions so strongly expressed on her wizened face. Edie's petite frame was supported by a mere five-foot stature, yet she filled the room with a voice of passion for her message. Every vocal exclamation was paired with talking hands. Rarely did they stop moving as she easily held her listeners' attention. Her thick Hungarian accent enhanced the validity of the story she told. And her hearty laugh occasionally broke free, amid tales of sorrow and unimaginable torture in Auschwitz.

Every step she took was a stride, larger than her short legs should be capable of taking. Sometimes she danced, brief minuets of grace. It gave me a glimpse into her past as an aspiring ballerina. Though she was seventy-three at the time, Edie resonated with the ability to do more than possibility implied, and I was riveted by her presence.

I lost track of time in her stories, feeling a kindred spirit, even while I understood my betrayal and confusion didn't compare with what she had endured. When the lunch break was announced, a line formed to greet Edie and shake hands with the dated woman in the tiny, powerhouse body. She sat queenlike in her chair and cordially shook hands with all who wanted to meet her.

I joined the line, landing somewhere in the middle. I've thought about this: I wasn't first, to explain her early interest. I wasn't last, causing her to linger. What happened next was the second miracle in my day.

We came face-to-face. Her voice, so vibrant on stage, became soft and warm. It spread over me like a healing balm. She dove into my pain-filled eyes with blue discerning pools of her own. When I offered my hand for a shake, she cupped it in a firm grip, covering the bottom of my hand with her right and the top with her left. The urgency in her voice was a shock. In an adamant Hungarian accent, she left no room for questioning her message or intent. "Ve must meet. You must have breakfast with me in the morning."

I could feel my eyes widen and my mouth gape. When the fullness of her demand registered in my brain, I responded, "But I don't live close. I'm almost two hours away."

"You must. God has spoken."

I'm sure I looked around to see if God was standing next to me and somehow I'd missed His regal presence. But He was not there in bodily form. It was only Edie in the chair, me standing in front of her, and the line of people behind me, stuck until we finished our exchange.

She gently pushed. "Child, ve must talk; you must meet me in the morning."

"I'll have to call my husband."

"Call, but it is ordained."

I wasn't sure how she could know such a thing— God certainly wasn't speaking to me—but I didn't question her authority. I nodded my head dumbly and hurried off to call my husband.

In the afternoon, when Edie had finished her session, I approached her nervously. By then I wondered if I had imagined our earlier interchange. Was I losing my mind?

But her welcoming smile assured me my memory was reality. Her movements had slowed from a long day of sharing emotional and inspiring words, but her passion still sparkled in her eyes. "So you vill come?"

"Yes. I will come."

I wrote down the directions to her hotel, and I agreed to meet her at eight in the morning. Somehow she had penetrated my ravaged heart with her unspoken understanding.

On the drive home, I marveled. More than three hundred people were in attendance that day, and yet she chose me. The miracles kept on coming.

Breakfast lasted more than three hours. Edie told me details I'd never read or heard about of atrocities in the Nazi prison camps—starvation, humiliation, cannibalism, emotional torture, mental games, physical maiming, and soul stripping. There was no part of the human existence left untouched by the cruel men and women who meted out the twisted desires of the SS.

Edie was only sixteen when she, her sister, mother, and father were ushered onto the stench-infused cattle car. Human beings were piled on top of each other, stacked high, in order to fit more bodies into each slatted square. Packed tightly so even the very attempt to breathe was not guaranteed. There was no regard for those on the bottom or stuffed into the far corners, those who most often died, some before the train ever pulled away from the station.

For days they traveled in claustrophobic quarters, their limbs cramped, tongues parched, lips cracked. Their bellies growled. Their bladders stretched. Their bowels gurgled. When human bodies finally released the intense pressures that built inside, there was no choice but to endure the shame of letting go within sight and hearing of their fellow passengers. Dignity was a thing of their past.

When the train steamed to a stop and their stiff arms, legs, necks, and torsos unfolded, relief was short-lived. Prodded by gunpoint, the prisoners formed a single line that seemed to stretch for miles. Over long hours, they inched their way forward, eyes to the ground.

Exhausted and numb, when Edie and her clan finally neared the head of the line, she could see a man seated in a stuffed chair. From his comfortable position, he would point at each new arrival who stood directly in front of him, branching the single line into two at its head. Right or left, the line broke into a human Y. Those who formed the Y couldn't question why. They had no choice—choice belonged solely to the man in the chair.

When Edie and her family took the final step into their fate, the well-dressed man pointed her and her sister into one line and her parents to the other. At the tender age of sixteen, Edie rushed to her mother, crying and clutching the older woman's arm.

The man eased from his chair and slowly made his way to the desperate girl. "Do not fret, little one. I am only sending you to the showers. Soon enough, you and your family will be together again." He gently pulled Edie from her mother and guided her back to the place he had originally directed.

Sniffling, Edie and her sister clung to each other, even as they looked tearfully over their shoulders, not wasting a single second that allowed them a glimpse of their father's shoulder or a wisp of their mother's hair. The comfort of a temporary separation, melded with a sisterly connection, was enough to get Edie through the rigorous cleaning and rough handling of her Nazi processing.

But hours later, as she and her sister wandered the foreign soil of the strange encampment, the fear and frustration of not finding their parents in a sea of humans took its toll. Clinging to each other as fresh hot tears tore down their faces, Edie looked up and through her hazy blur saw an old man in a prison uniform approaching.

"Little girls, why do you cry?"

Edie, being the eldest, spoke for them both. "Our ma-ma, our pa-pa. Ve cannot find them anywhere. The man in the chair. He told us ve vould be reunited after our showers. But ve have looked for the longest time, and ve have searched from one fence to the other."

"Ah. Mengele. Ve call him the angel of death. He is a great liar, that one." The old man pointed with a gnarled finger at a pair of tall, brick-red smokestacks. "There is your ma-ma. There is your pa-pa. The Nazis. They have killed them both."

Riveted by Edie's personal account, not knowing how long I had cried, I noticed the puddle on the table below my face. I thought of my own painful history, so recent, so raw, but knowing it was nothing compared to what this woman across from me had endured. And yet she smiled, while I could not.

Edie switched subjects on me. Deftly she asked me soft questions about my own story. "Why is the pain etched so deeply around your eyes? What hurts directed God to tell me to meet with you?"

I told her about the fear I had harbored for years because of past wounds. The thing that terrified me more than cancer, more than hunger, and more than death. I was scared that my husband would commit adultery. Gasping for air, I told her my worst fears had come true. I confessed how much I wanted to die.

Edie let me sob until there were no more tears to rip from my tattered soul. She rubbed my hands, and with salty pools at the edges of her own blue eyes, she clucked comforting words over me. "There, there, my child. There, there."

The waitress approached our table cautiously. "Would you ladies like something more to drink? It's nearing lunchtime." She glanced toward the wall clock. "Would you care to order another meal?"

I looked at my half-eaten omelet but pushed it farther away. The thought of food repulsed me. Refusing to show our server my puffy face, I looked at the buttons on her blouse and said, "I'd like some more iced tea, please."

"Sure, sweetie." I hated the pity dripping off her words.

Edie waved her away with a hand of dismissal. "Just more vater."

The waitress must have read the message that food or drink was not our main objective. She dipped her head in a show of respect and said, "Sure." Then she scurried away.

Edie wasted no time in moving the conversation away from my meltdown. "Let me tell you of another event in Auschwitz."

I sniffled and nodded my head for her to continue.

"Somehow, Mengele learned of my aspiration to become a great ballerina. He summoned me before him. He forced me to dance for him and his top officials. It pained me greatly to entertain the monster who had stolen the lives of my mother and father. The beast who had destroyed many innocent people. But if I did not, I knew I vould die. A part of me velcomed death, but something stronger fought its arrival."

My head bobbed up and down. I understood her love-hate description at the thought of death and dying.

"Vhen I finished the last pirouette, he surprised me with a precious reward. A full loaf of bread. Not the moldy, hardened crusts of our daily rations, but a soft, warm, plump loaf that I could have all to myself.

"After he released me back to my dormitory, I

hugged the bread to my breast. My heart pounded with my footsteps—I felt as if I were seated at a king's feast and had been treated as the guest of honor.

"When I entered the bleak shack that was the housing area for me and half a dozen other women, my thoughts battled within me. Should I keep the bread to myself, cherishing its nourishment for several days, making it last as long as possible? I could secret it away, where they would not see me in the dark of night, gnawing like a mouse who stumbles on a brick of rich cheese.

"But vhat of the other vomen who shared my misery? Vas it fair that I should receive a priceless gift while their bellies suffered and clenched in agony? It vas not their fault that my dancing should offer so great a reward. I could not explain my good fortune, but neither could I keep it to myself.

"I called my imprisoned sisters to huddle around me and then unveiled vhat I had to offer. The oohs and aahs comforted my mind and assured me the choice I'd made had been right. Ve feasted in awe that evening, celebrating together. I did not know that this single decision vould later save my life."

While Edie took a break to sip some water, I realized I was so enraptured by her story that while she spoke, my mind was distracted from my own problems. The relief, mixed with intrigue and compassion, made me antsy for her to pick up where she'd left off.

Edie cleared her throat and took another draw from her water glass. When she placed it back on the table, I noticed the precision with which she aligned it exactly where it had been on the coaster. "Several months later, near starvation, my little loaf of bread vas no more. The crumbs in my memory vere all that remained."

I scooted closer to the table.

"At first ve didn't know the Allies vere getting close. But something had changed. There vas an urgency in the vay the Nazis ushered us out of the camp. Ve vere used to the frigid air the thin boards and vide cracks in our housing units let in. But the blasts that pummeled our bodies as ve began the death march felt like hot pokers against our exposed skin."

I don't think Edie noticed the way she rubbed both of her arms, as if the biting cold from her past had invaded our present. But I saw.

"Ve stumbled for hours through the night and the day. But ve dared not fall. The echo of a rifle shot exploding in our ears and the sharp smell of gunpowder that singed our nostrils alerted us to each poor soul whose body could take no more.

"I eventually became numb to the sense of cold, but my own limbs vere varning me with each new step. I struggled to lift my feet, and my ankles were not cooperating as I needed. I knew the end was near and prayed it would happen swiftly. I vas so very tired.

"But then, a miracle.

"I do not know who took the courage to ask. I do not know vhy the guards allowed it. But the vomen with whom I'd shared my loaf of bread vere given permission to make a chair with their arms. I do not know how long they carried me, but it was enough to allow me to regain a parcel of strength. Enough for me to make it to the edge of the city.

"It was there I collapsed.

"Overcome with starvation and exhaustion, I could push my body no more. They thought I had expired, and so I vas thrown onto a pile of dead bodies at the edge of the street. I could not protest. Veakness overpowered me so I could not shift away from the putrid odor of rotted flesh."

I swiped my cheek with a paper napkin, and Edie cleared the gravel from her voice box. Her voice had softened to just above a whisper when she spoke again. "Vhatever eternity vaited for me, I could no longer question."

I swallowed hard at the instant dryness filling my mouth.

"Soon after, vhen the Allies arrived, an American soldier patrolling in his Jeep spotted the slightest movement of my finger in the pile. He stopped immediately, got out, and pulled me to safety. This is vhy I came to America. He is vhy I now call it my home. He is vhy I became a doctor of psychology." She pierced me with a lasered look, and her voice strengthened. "He is the one God sent so I could live. There vas purpose yet to be fulfilled, and my ultimate destiny could come only through my darkness."

I marveled at the confidence and peace echoing beneath her words. I couldn't imagine surviving such loss and yet gaining such deep hope.

She cocked her head at me, as if she could read my thoughts. When she spoke, I was almost sure she had. "You might vonder how my experience could possibly speak to yours."

I'm sure I nodded the affirmative.

"You know the Twenty-Third Psalm. Yes?"

I nodded again.

"So you are avare of the vording, 'Yea, though I valk through the valley of the shadow of death.' Are you not?"

"Yes, of course."

"You must pay attention to the intent of His words. Notice it does not say, 'Slow down.' It does not say, 'Stop.' It does not say, 'Pitch a tent.' It does not say, 'Build a house.' It says, 'Valk.' "

She leaned as far as her slight body would allow over the table toward me. "In the darkness, you may feel you cannot valk. When you are very tired, you will believe you cannot go on. But these are lies. You can. And you must. You must place one foot forward each day, taking one tiny step at a time. Do not vorry that you cannot see far ahead of you. Simply step."

I could feel the passion in her words releasing adrenaline into my muscles.

"Vhen you think you vill collapse from exhaustion, you remember me. See my face in your mind, as you see me now. Think of my story. And then valk. Vhen you are sure you have no strength left, place one foot on the ground in front of you. Just one in that moment. And as you remember vhat my friends did for me, remember that God offers His strength to carry you farther than you can go on your own."

She reached across and gripped both of my hands in hers but never turned her intense sky-blue gaze away from my eyes.

"I promise you. One day you vill be surprised to find that you stepped out of the valley of darkness into the light once again. It vill stop you vhere you stand in that moment of clarity. You vill turn and look back into the valley, but the light will separate you from the dark hurts of your past.

"Though it is hard to believe now, you vill smile once again. The flavor of foods vill return to your palette. You vill breathe deep of the scents in the vind. You vill brush the velvet texture of newly blushed rose petals. The serenade of birds will sing joy to your soul."

She drew an inspirational picture, but I agreed with her—as much as my heart ached for everything she described, I could not fathom a day I would ever feel a breath of happiness again.

But I was wrong.

My breakfast with Dr. Edie Eger lasted all day. I drove her to the airport for her late afternoon flight. While we stood outside the terminal, she laid her hands on my cheeks as if she were touching fragile butterfly wings. "There is a vounded little girl inside of you who needs a mother. You mother her." And then she hugged me close in a final goodbye.

If I looked the way I felt, my sobs appeared as if they belonged in a six-year-old little girl's body, though I was a grown woman. But even then, I knew this day had changed me. I would never be the same. It would take much time. I would endure many more days of grief. But I would remember the woman from Auschwitz who walked. And because of her, I would do the same.

I won't lie to you: it took many excruciating steps, and I often imagined Edie's death march to get through what I knew I would never get over. But one tiny inch at a time, there came a day when I experienced what she promised. I can't tell you precisely when, but I can recall the moment when it surprised me to realize I was not only smiling but laughing. I had stepped out of the valley into the light.

Long before I felt better, as a result of my one encounter with Edie, I braved a life-changing decision. I chose to love as if I'd never been hurt. I had to rededicate myself to that determination many times over. But through practice my feelings eventually followed my faith in what I could not yet see and had not yet experienced but trusted would happen.

It took both my husband and me walking toward the same destination of healing—but we never gave up, and today we are a couple transformed. Our marriage is the result of an influencer in a tiny, wizened body. A woman who overcame unspeakable torture, but never gave up.

Edie endured the atrocities and daily betrayals of a Nazi war camp, and she used that experience to make a difference in the world instead of wallowing in her misery. Her example meant I could not excuse myself. I must allow God to transform my mess into a message of hope.

The stories you will read through the rest of this book, true accounts of people who were forced to face some of their greatest fears, only exist because of the endurance that grew through deep valley hikes. People who understand Job's determination in Job 13:15 where he says, "Though he slay me, yet will I trust in him" (KJV). On these pages, I pray their marches inspire and strengthen you to take steps of your own.

But I must add an important piece of professional advice. If while reading this book you feel triggered by inner stress or anxiety and find yourself agitated and/or drawn to harm yourself, drink excessively, overeat, disassociate, or zone out, it's a sign things are being stirred too quickly. According to licensed professional counselor Lucille Zimmerman (www.lucillezimmerman.com), you should immediately take a break, go for a walk, or call a friend, and hopefully see a counselor as soon as possible.

She also suggests telling your own story to at least one safe person. As Lucille says, "Shame dies when light is shone on it. Since we get hurt in relationships, we usually need to heal in relationship." Just exercise caution about whom you share your private details with.

Though God doesn't cause tragedy, He is willing to carry us through it. He can transform our ashes into a crown of beauty and each of our messes into life-changing messages of hope. As you turn the pages of this book and experience the stories of others' heartaches,

I pray you are strengthened and encouraged to walk through your own dark circumstances. You may not get *over* your pain, but with help and encouragement, you will eventually get *through* it and one day step back into the light of joy.

INSIDER INSIGHTS

Emotional Healing

- Incorporate uplifting music into your healing plan. The vibrations in song resonate with the chords in our souls, so choose wisely. Pick soft melodies, words of praise and gratitude, encouraging messages blanketed with instrumental harmonies and empowering lyrics. All of these will assist, as God transforms your mourning into dancing. One of my favorite healing songs is Matt Redman's "You Never Let Go." Knowing we don't travel the valley alone gives us the strength to get through. Sing the words out loud, trusting before you see the results of your faith.

- Traumatic experiences often require the help of a professional guide to support us through our healing process. Searching for a counselor whose value system matches your own and with whom you feel safe can make a critical difference in the speed and depth of your healing.

- When you are ready, connecting with at least one healthy person in your everyday life offers ongoing mentoring possibilities. A word of caution: do not use your friends as a mental crutch. I simply suggest in the natural flow of friendship, godly counsel from someone who knows you well and is willing to offer honest feedback can be invaluable between professional visits.

Practical Help

- Get outside and go for walks in the fresh air when you can. The healing benefits of exercise while breathing in plant-generated oxygen aids in healing the body, mind, and spirit.
- Drink water. You may wonder how this helps, but hydration reduces foggy brain syndrome and helps us control deceptive emotions.
- Schedule rest, and maintain consistent sleep habits. When we are fatigued, it is almost impossible to process our feelings in a healthy way. Forcing your body to adjust to a regular pattern of going to bed at the same time will eventually move you past insomnia.

Spiritual Comfort

- Remember that one of the names for the Holy Spirit in the Greek is Paraclete. It means "advocate, comforter, encourager, or counselor" (see the word *Helper* in the next scripture reference). This aspect of God's character offers you counseling money can't buy. Jesus said in John 16:7, "But I tell you the truth, it is better for you that I go away. When I go away, I will send the Helper to you. If I do not go away, the Helper will not come" (NCV).

- "Consider it pure joy, my brothers and sisters, whenever you face trials of many kinds, because you know that the testing of your faith produces perseverance. Let perseverance finish its work so that you may be mature and complete, not lacking anything" (James 1:2–4).

- "Even when I walk through the darkest valley, I will not be afraid, for you are close beside me. Your rod and your staff protect and comfort me" (Psalm 23:4 NLT).

GUIDED PRAYER

Dear God,

Though the valley is black, in faith I trust You to shine the way. Though I am weak, I praise You in advance for lending me Your strength. Though I fear I will never get through, I thank You for giving me the courage to believe. By Your power, I will walk, taking one faith-filled step at a time, until one day soon, You deliver me into the light.

CHAPTER 2

Little Girl Lost

PTSD. Could it be affecting you?

This term is quickly becoming a buzzword, in danger of being viewed as a cliché—overlooked, overused, and underappreciated. But what is PTSD, and does it affect the everyday person?

Dr. Phillip C. McGraw, known internationally as Dr. Phil, describes PTSD this way: "A complex anxiety disorder that may develop after exposure to an extremely stressful or life-threatening event."[1]

According to *Merriam-Webster Dictionary*, the medical definition of post-traumatic stress disorder is this: "A psychological reaction occuring after experiencing a highly stressing event (as wartime combat, physical violence, or a natural disaster) that is usually characterized by depression, anxiety, flashbacks, recurrent nightmares, and avoidance of reminders of the event—abbreviation *PTSD*; called also *post-traumatic stress syndrome*."

I am not a professional clinician, and I have no ability or desire to diagnose PTSD or any other mental health occurrence. However, I am an everyday person who has survived much pain, interviewed PTSD victims, researched the subject extensively, spoken with credentialed experts, and explored the possibility that growing numbers of people are touched by it.

With twenty-first-century technology, we are exposed directly or indirectly to increased incidents of violence in schools, movie theaters, workplaces, and shopping malls. Add to this buried childhood trauma, and I can't help but wonder how many of us have the symptoms and don't recognize them. If physical and emotional signs are any indication, I venture to guess many of us are hampered by our past experiences.

Through this book, I hope to shed light and offer hope regarding a subject affecting many. My desire to do so in layman terms, breaking things down to an understandable level for the everyday person, stems from an unshakable belief that it's never too late for a fresh start with fresh faith.

But to find relief from any problem, I've learned we must recognize, acknowledge, and act differently than we have before. We cannot continue in stale habits, expecting new results. If we are to break the chains that bind us, the clouds that hover over us, and the numbness that hides our true and beautiful selves, we must take courage and get honest. The truth *will* set us free.

My studies lead me to believe that one of the most invasive and common causes of PTSD hides beneath the mask of normal-looking people. Both women and men are susceptible.

According to the Rape, Abuse & Incest National Network (RAINN), every two minutes someone in the United States is sexually assaulted. Sixty percent of these assaults are never reported. Two-thirds are committed by someone known by the victim. Eighty percent of the victims are under the age of thirty.

These facts breed high odds for PTSD occurrence. Jill's story below shows us how a single incident can change a life, wreaking havoc long after we believe we've buried it in the past and left it far behind.

Jill was five when it happened to her. For some who are used this way, abuse happens when they're younger; some are more mature. But does age matter when it comes to emotional trauma?

Jill's golden-brown waves bounced and reflected the summer sun—her hazel eyes on the lookout for new fun and adventures. She played in her open backyard, oblivious to the evil lurking a few steps away. She would often lie on her back, shielding her eyes from bright sunlight, while she looked for animals embedded in the puffy clouds above her head.

Her family was poor, maybe not dirt poor, but dusty. At this stage in her life, she wore only dresses, hand-me-downs from compassionate women at the church. Most hung on her skinny frame just below gnarly knees. Jill was a tomboy. With no interest in dolls, she played with Matchbox cars on roads constructed with bare hands.

But her favorite pastime was clawing up scratchy brown bark to sit as high as she could climb, until hidden, she swayed on leaf-covered limbs. Sometimes she'd scramble up an apple or peach tree, plucking a tart fruit. Her little cheeks puckered at the first juicy bite.

She thought birds must feel like this, high in the

sky, free on the wind, eyeing faraway places, safe, and close to God. She had only recently begun to wonder who God was and what He might think of her.

In those quiet moments, she talked privately with Him, a practice she would soon need as she was propelled into an unimaginable maze of confusion for a preschool mind. It would take her a lifetime to get through many twists and turns, the effects making her forget she had been carried into a darkness she did not choose.

Jill, an outdoor girl, shrouded in the shades of nature and colors of the rainbow, felt cradled in a blanket of security. Every once in a while her mommy would holler out the back door, "Jill, where are you?"

"Here," she would say.

"Just checking."

The world around her offered protective reassurance, and earthy scents filled Jill with relaxation and sweet happiness.

It was this trusting little girl who answered a beckoning call from a neighbor boy. Brother to the actual perpetrator—a sixteen-year-old who stole her innocence, plenty old enough to know better.

"Come here." He grinned from behind the fence post.

"Un-uh." She shook her wild brown curls in response.

"I won't hurt you." He waved his hand in a come-hither motion.

"Un-uh," she repeated.

"I've got something you'll want to see."

Strong curiosity gripped her in that instant.

He lifted his right hand and shook it back and forth, the glint of gold flashing in a sunray.

She took a cautious step toward the fence line.

His black head bobbed encouragement. "That's it. But you can't see it very good from there. Come closer." Only eleven himself, he was doing his brother's bidding. But he did it well.

She looked around, as if the answer would show up, maybe scrawled on the ground. Was this okay?

"It's really pretty. See?" He waved the skinny golden scepter over the wire fence.

Drawn like a magnet, Jill couldn't turn back—and she no longer wanted to. What she wanted was the pretty object in the older boy's hand. Arriving at the silver squares of fence separating their property lines, she stood at least a foot shorter than he. She looked up, squinting from the afternoon harshness in the sky, and all she could make out clearly was gold. The gold she wanted so desperately.

"Wanna hold it?"

She held out her delicate little hand, and he dropped the shiny gold ink pen into her pink palm. An adult would see it as ordinary, but to a poor little five-year-old, it was magical.

She turned, twisted, and rolled the fine instrument and felt the heat of it push into her flesh. "Can I have it?" Jill looked up sheepishly, even while she dared a delicate bare foot onto one of the fence squares. The step up caused her chin to poke past the boundary onto the other side.

"Sure, but you have to do something." He snatched the pen from her fingers.

Jill's stomach sank, and she immediately felt nauseous at the loss. She nodded her head—desperate to get the golden ink pen back.

"Meet me at the end of your garden, and I'll tell you what you have to do. Then you can keep it."

A five-year-old doesn't know the consequence of selling her soul for an ink pen, but Jill was about to learn. Unthinking, she ran to get her prize.

It took no more than two or three minutes for her to slash through cornstalks taller than her head, but in Jill's angst to regain a precious treasure, it felt like forever. It hurt to want something so bad.

They met at the end of the large garden planted several yards away from her house. Almost out of view. Somewhere Mommy had told her not to go.

"Come over here." The boy stood a few feet beyond his own boundary line.

"I'm not supposed to."

"No one will know."

Daddy and Mommy had warned numerous times, "Never cross our fence line." But surely the boy was right. She could hop on over, grab her gold, and be back before she ever got caught. Still, she hesitated.

"You want it, don't you?" he taunted her again.

She couldn't take it anymore. She scaled the fence, and he helped her down the other side. He ran toward the woods, and she followed, excitement pounding in her heart.

Just into the thick oak trees, she saw him. The bigger boy. She stopped cold. Her small feet skittered on dead leaves. Dread crept from her bowels up her throat.

The smile on his face was dead. His eyes were of medium color but dark in appearance, void of humanity. "Don't be afraid, I won't hurt you."

Jill didn't believe him, and she wanted to run. A burning in her legs begged her to turn and take off, but she was paralyzed. Rooted where she had skidded to a stop.

"Why don't you help her out?" His voice had a stickiness to it, and it made her feel like vomiting.

The younger brother obliged, gently nudging her shoulder toward the big, scary body seated on the ground at the foot of a thick tree trunk.

"That's it," he coaxed with honeyed cooing.

Everything deep inside of her wanted to fight. Wanted to run. Wanted to scream. Wanted to escape. Yet Jill felt powerless, as if someone had wrapped her in a strong cocoon, where she could see. But Jill couldn't move without assistance.

The brother inched her closer without her feet lifting off the forest floor.

When she was close enough, the big boy reached out and grabbed her arms. His steely grip seemed to burn holes in her cotton sleeves. He eased her to the ground directly in front of him. The earth didn't smell comforting there—it reeked of fear and evil. His touch hurt before she should have felt physical pain.

A slippery smile slithered across his mouth. "Mmm, that's nice." Spittle pooled at the edges of his lips. His breath stank of unbrushed teeth.

Jill ground her jaws and bit the inside of her cheek—anything so she wouldn't cry. But her words still came out wobbly. "I want to go home."

"Sure. In a minute." He leered, and she looked away.

He reached to draw her onto his slimy lap, but then. . .a voice shouted from beyond the tree line.

"Jilly, where are you?" She could hear the worry from Mommy as she used her family nickname.

"My mommy wants me."

The perpetrator's eyes widened, and he let go. He and his brother exchanged scowls.

While they were busy looking at each other, Jill scrambled off the ground, pulling her underwear back in place. She took off running. She didn't dare look back, terrified that if she did, one of their huge, groping hands would catch her and pull her back into the woods.

While she sprinted, Mommy kept calling, "Where are you?" Jill could hear panic start to vibrate her mom's vocal chords. "Answer me, Jilly. Do you hear me? Answer me."

Heaving for breath, sweat pouring off her anxiety-ridden body, Jill didn't stop until she stood in the shadow of her mother's tall frame. Worry turned her mommy's eyebrows into a V as she looked down. "Where were you?"

Jill couldn't tell her she'd crossed the fence line. Jill felt sick because she had wanted the gold ink pen so badly. Mommy always said not to treat things as more important than people.

Shame seeped into every pore of her being. Inside and out, she trembled at the realization of what kind of person she really was. It was her fault this bad thing happened.

"Well? Where were you?"

Jill looked down at her bare feet. "Nowhere."

"You were somewhere. Why didn't you answer me when I called?"

"I don't know."

"Look at me when I'm talking to you."

Before she complied, Jill watched her tears splatter muddy prints along her dusty toe tops. Then she looked up very slowly. "I'm okay, Mommy."

When their eyes met, Mommy leaned down and squeezed Jill so tight it made what little air she had left in her lungs whoosh out in a gush. When she was able to breathe in, her mother's familiar smell oozed comfort and safety through the fabric of her shirt. Mommy sobbed and clutched Jill closer.

They stayed that way for several long seconds; then Mommy pulled away and drilled Jill with hazel eyes that looked like a bigger version of Jill's own. "You scared me to death. You don't know what can happen to little girls."

Jill nodded her little head up and down in silent agreement. Sadly, Mommy didn't realize Jill had gotten her first lesson. At five years old, she shivered as a flashback from minutes earlier crossed her mind, the beginning of many she would endure into adulthood.

For years after, Jill wrestled with this memory. Sometimes she successfully pinned it in her subconscious for a season of life, but then it would slither out. Fuzzy dreams would bother her for days, even when she couldn't recall the details or what it was that made her feel awful. She often couldn't identify why she felt a gray cloud over her head or had the blahs.

As an adult, food addictions and an intrinsic drive to treat herself poorly were ongoing foes. She knew she should exercise, eat healthy, and get enough rest. Yet she battled with an inner demon who desired to destroy her from the inside out.

This haunting ghost attempted to convince her of her grunginess, her lack of value. He told Jill she was a failure, someone who got what she deserved then—someone who continued to deserve punishment now. Because of what happened to her when she was five years old, Jill fought to believe anything good could or should happen to her as an adult. Even after the healing impact of good therapy, she had to remain vigilant against her propensity for self-destructive behaviors.

In hindsight, after years of trying to escape the memory, to force it into her subconscious, staying busy in hopes of outrunning it, Jill realized how much this first sexual trauma affected her. Its impact lingered through symptoms of PTSD. Counseling revealed how deeply she was terrorized and how helpless she'd felt in those moments when someone bigger, stronger, and older forced his will on her. For years Jill wondered why she had an ongoing struggle with four specific areas.

- eating disorders
- a compulsive need to control
- panic attacks
- sexual anxiety with her husband

Through long-term therapy, Jill learned she overate as a way to shroud herself in what she subconsciously hoped was an unattractive covering. Somewhere in the depth of buried fear and worry, she thought this might protect her from new attacks.

The helplessness Jill experienced as a five-year-old at the hands of a forceful perpetrator threw her into the role of vigilant controller. Always on guard, afraid to trust her well-being to anyone else, she developed a pattern of protection through controlling habits.

In her young-adult years, a different kind of trauma triggered an onset of panic attacks—some mild, others debilitating. In the process of professional counseling, along with private prayer and meditation, Jill discovered the connection to her severe anxiety went beyond recent events, and it was rooted at the core of her sexual abuse.

Jill loved her husband. But when it came to expressions of physical affection, she often locked up. She couldn't explain why—to her husband or herself. In the years she avoided the truth of her sexual abuse, her ability to relax and enjoy a natural relationship with her husband was especially hampered.

Until she squared off face-to-face with her past, the source of her earliest sense of shame, Jill wasn't free to unbolt the chains that held her and her mate captive. Once she stood up to her history, it no longer held the power of making her feel as if it were repeated when she was with her husband. She was released to experience the beauty of a fulfilling sex life in the purity of her marriage bed.

To reach a place of healing, Jill first had to acknowledge the truth. She has since gotten through the impact of childhood sexual abuse, even though she will never get over it.

But sometimes we bury our past so deep even we have trouble finding where we put it. There's a prevailing sense that things are off, something perpetually gnaws at us from the inside, though we can't pinpoint what it is. So we need help to unearth the mounds of dirt piled over our past.

There are two particular methods I've found helpful in my own work and personal life to identify the core of emotional paralysis, those things that make me ask these questions:

"Why can't I get out of this rut?"

"I know better. So why do I keep doing this to myself?"

"Is this all there is to life?"

"Does God just hate me?"

Poor patterns cause us to make the same mistakes

over and over again, usually with the hope that we will get new results. We don't want to feel this way. We don't want to set ourselves up for failure. Yet some of us follow a predictable cycle of self-induced negativity—habits that make us feel bad not only about what we do or don't do but about who we are.

Maybe you can relate. Maybe you know someone else who can.

Guilt is a powerful adversary, even when it's unfounded—even when you have Christ. We often confuse shame and guilt. Shame is directly tied to who we are, while guilt is directly tied to what we do. Shame is unhealthy, while healthy guilt can spur us to learn from our mistakes and make better decisions in the future. But assistance may be required to help us figure out what causes false guilt and why we feel ashamed.

Again, I recommend professional help, but within the support system of appropriate therapy, I have found two processes beneficial in unveiling the true cause of my own issues.

- *Brainstorming.* As a certified training facilitator, I first used this exercise in workplace settings, discovering how powerful it was in freeing the mind to find the real source of problems. Once you know where you need to focus attention, through this simple yet effective method, you can then flow into highly creative solutions. After I saw the benefits organizations received, I tweaked the steps and tried it on a personal level. By giving myself permission to let my mind run unfettered, it drew covered memories out into the open. Sometimes, days or weeks after I started the process, bits and pieces bubbled to the surface of my conscience. Once identified, I could begin the healing process. The key is to write down your insights; generating a mental list is not enough. I offer basic brainstorming guidelines on my website at http://anitabrooks.com/brainstorming-guidelines-tips-from-a-certified-facilitator.

- *Storyboarding*. Visual aids enhance our ability to see things we would otherwise miss. Storyboarding is something you can do for nearly no cost, takes a matter of minutes, and can be done in one sitting or off and on over a period of weeks, but it could positively change the way you see and react to your own life. With nothing more than paper, pen, and authorization from yourself to go there, draw a timeline of your life from birth to present. For specific steps, ideas, and photo examples, go to this link: http://anitabrooks.com/storyboarding-for-success.

More than four decades ago, five-year-old little Jill quaked in the aftermath of a life-changing trauma. But today her laughter tinkles from inside a woman's adult body. From time to time, she allows herself to frolic and play. She's gotten through it.

But it doesn't mean there aren't periodic bouts where painful memories force her to work hard again. When the memories come, it takes much less time for her emotions to simmer down from a boiling point. She knows how to face the pain and take specific actions to help her process and deal with her reality in a healthy way, until finally she's able to feel relief and happiness once again. Little Jill, in big Jill's body, celebrates her full life often.

I wonder if you can identify with Jill's story. Are you searching for relief and happiness, afraid you'll never experience them again? Or maybe you've buried painful memories in crevices so deep you think they've gone away. And yet there's a pervasive cloud, a smothering that won't allow you to let loose and laugh, to enjoy the fullness of living.

If you can relate, then maybe you'll benefit from the comfort offered in this book. But prepare yourself for difficult moments.

If an uncomfortable memory is stirred, try not to run from it unless a professional guide confirms that it might be dangerous for you to face it. Otherwise, take a brief rest, then pick up courage, intentionally acknowledge and work through all parts of your unresolved past, and propel yourself to a place of deeper joy.

Remember Edie, and march on.

According to experts in the field, the following warning signs can alert us to the possibility we have serious and unfinished business hindering our ability to live a peace-filled, abundant, and happy life.

- troubling dreams or nightmares—especially recurring ones
- intrusive recollections—where a painful memory keeps coming back and disrupts normal activities
- reliving trauma as illusions, hallucinations, and dissociative flashbacks
- intense psychological distress at exposure to cues—an abnormal response triggered by a particular sight, sound, or smell
- physiological reaction to cues—physical symptoms such as consistent bouts of headaches, nausea, minor illnesses, backaches, eating disorders, substance addictions, and more
- avoiding thoughts, feelings, or conversations—burying memories, emotions, or anything else you attach to a traumatic event, and refusing to discuss or relive them with another person
- avoiding activities, places, or people—hiding from known triggers that might force you to face a memory
- feelings of detachment—believing you should experience certain emotions, particularly those of affection, attachment, concern, or compassion, while unable to feel them appropriately
- irritable or aggressive behavior—angry responses that leave you as well as others confused at the reason and/or intensity of your reactions

The US Department of Veterans Affairs website, www.ptsd.va.gov/understand/types_sexual_trauma_child.asp, tells us survivors of sexual abuse, left untreated, are prone to these symptoms:

- PTSD and anxiety
- depression and thoughts of suicide
- sexual anxiety and disorders, including having too many or unsafe sexual partners
- difficulty setting safe limits with others (e.g., saying no to people) and relationship problems
- poor body image and low self-esteem
- unhealthy behaviors, such as abuse of alcohol or drugs, self-harm, or eating problems. These behaviors are often used to hide painful emotions related to the abuse.

Again, see a therapist right away if you believe unfinished business from your past exposes you to the above-mentioned symptoms. To help you, here's a list of points to remember when it comes to seeking professional counsel:

- Just because someone has credentials doesn't mean he or she is the right fit to lead you out of your emotional imprisonment. Do your homework; research their educational and experiential claims.
- Use common sense and get second or third opinions if things don't feel right. Not everything we're told is good for us.

- Find someone whose values match your own. Human beings are more easily influenced than we recognize, especially when it comes to exploring sensitive issues. Don't waste time, energy, and money, only to figure out later you were led down a rabbit trail in an area that doesn't align with your ethics or moral boundaries.

Many events jerk the rug out from under our feet when it comes to beliefs in the world we thought we could trust. In our next chapter, we'll explore shocking news related to questions of identity. Learning this kind of truth is more common than you think and something people definitely don't get over.

INSIDER INSIGHTS

Emotional Healing

- How many of us don't need the power and promise of resurrection after an emotional death—a reminder that our abuse is over now and we survived for a reason? Matthew West's inspiring song "Broken Girl" speaks a truth every former abused child needs to hear. Note I used the word *former*. From this moment on, you are not defined by your past.
- Find a person who's a soft place to land where you can safely vent. Look for a soothing environment, like a church, a thinking tree, a large rock by a river or lake, or a walking trail.

Seek any consistent place where you can face your past in a safe zone. Try to spend a minimum of fifteen minutes twice a week reliving, spewing, releasing—or whatever healthy way you can adopt to get the poisons out.

- Spend five minutes every day with an intentional focus on trying to capture one *happy* childhood memory. Focus on the details—the smell, the taste, the sounds, the textures, as well as the sights. So much of sexual trauma revolves around reliving or expending volumes of energy trying to avoid thinking about that moment that changed our lives forever. But I've found one simple solution—we can only think of one distinct, detailed thought at a time. So changing direction and focusing on a happy thought gives us bouts of relief from dwelling on hurtful events we could not control.

Practical Help

- Make solitude an everyday habit. Give yourself the gift of temporary silence. Maybe it's a warm bath with the door locked so the kids can't get in. You might want to invest in soundproofing earplugs to block the noises of ordinary family living for this special time.
- Read something inspiring, healing, and/or educational.
- Journal by writing out your story as you

remember it. Be as graphic and detailed as possible. Allow yourself to cry, shout, scream, and vent at your perpetrator through the process. Afterward, burn or bury your hurt in the ground. The important thing is to remove the unresolved grief stuck inside you and feel what you need to feel. Get what's inside outside. This is where true healing begins.

Spiritual Comfort

- Go to Jesus when you are drawn into pain-infused memories or covered in that yucky feeling you can't quite identify the origin of. Imagine Him holding your hand, looking at you with a huge, accepting smile and a look of love that crinkles the edges of His eyes. Hear Him say, "As the Father has loved me, so have I loved you. Now remain in my love" (John 15:9).

- Read at least fifteen minutes in the Bible every day. Find a translation you connect to. In our twenty-first century, we are blessed to have many options at our disposal. If the King James Version doesn't read smoothly for you, then try the New International Version or New Living Translation. For a softer or more emotional read, try *The Message*, a paraphrased version. If you really want to have fun, compare multiple translations at once. Look up definitions to enrich your understanding. Make a game of finding all the fresh insights available to you. Let God speak directly to you and your pain through His personal love letter.

• One of the gnarly side effects of sexual abuse is feeling dirty and gross. But know that with God, all things are possible. He can do the unimaginable. With Him, it is finished. He can take the filthy places and make them clean—believe Him. " 'What God has made clean you must not say is unclean' " (Acts 10:15 NLV).

GUIDED PRAYER

Dear Jesus,

I'm scared to trust after what's happened to me, but I'm making a decision to believe You will love me purely, without seeing my stains. So I thank You in advance for helping me feel what I'm choosing to have faith in, that I am already clean because of the word You have spoken to me.

CHAPTER 3

Who's Your Daddy?

I t's more prevalent than we think.

One-third of American children grow up without their biological fathers, according to the US Census Bureau.[2] In the United Kingdom, one million men, 10.3 percent of all British fathers, don't live with their children.[3] In the past fifty years, nations around the globe have seen a staggering increase in children and adults affected by an identity void, forced to live with unknown or unrequited pieces of their biology.

Regardless of the reason for absenteeism, there's no escaping the fact that unanswered questions about our biology impact us as adults. Those affected often don't connect daily emotional struggles, patterns of self-destructive behaviors, and the inability to push past invisible barriers as direct links to post-traumatic stress symptoms rooted in a missing biological parent.

You don't get over death, divorce, abandonment, or an unidentified parent. But it is possible to get through. As Troy Dunn, better known as The Locator, says, "You can't find peace until you find all the pieces."[4]

Most people take their identity for granted—nationality, extended family, siblings, mom, and dad. However, a growing segment around the world are facing an existential crisis.

Sperm donors, surrogate mothers, out-of-country adoptions, rape, sexual promiscuity, parenting by same-sex partners, single parenting, and more have caused an increase in people who've never met one or both of their biological parents. While some may not care to know them, most children raised by nonblood parents have at least a mild curiosity, if only for health information. But the majority of men and women I've spoken with are compelled to search; they can't turn off their curiosity.

Another interesting aspect of identity crisis is how it makes you feel regardless of physical maturity. Grown men and women with children and grandchildren of their own have said to me, "When I let myself think about it, it's like I become a small child again. I can't explain why, but the thought of my birth mother or father makes me feel scared and helpless. It's like I lose all adult logic."

From my travels as an international speaker, I believe more people than ever are discovering their biological heritage wasn't what they thought. With DNA advances, there is certainly an increase in verifiable cases. "Who's your daddy?" isn't a funny slang saying for someone who doesn't really know the answer to the question.

When this kind of news is revealed later in life, things you took for granted are now confusing. Everyone is stunned. And a swell of people want to offer their opinions on your situation.

"Focus on your blessings."

"You have a mom/dad/grandma/grandpa/aunt/

uncle, etc., who loves you."

It's easy for someone secure in their ancestry to make these statements. But for those haunted by questions and blindsided by intrusive thoughts triggered by everyday occurrences they don't want to think about yet can't shut down, the feelings are painful.

If this describes you, you may spend your time numbing out, trying to make the unknown go away. Or the opposite. You may obsess and fall prey to panicky feelings, threatening to keep you from functioning at a seminormal level. Bouncing between symptoms of identity trauma can smother you with deep shame. You may feel like you're losing it. Everything's in question. You wonder if you're a mistake.

Sometimes the answers to plaguing questions come from strange places. That's what happened to me one Sunday evening.

"It's okay to be alive." Some viewers may have missed the statement by Scott Pelley, *60 Minutes* commentator, interviewing a postwar soldier on the latest PTSD treatments.[5] But there was a reason it caught my ear. Like all humans, I'm hardwired with a driving burn to know where I come from. Why do I exist? Do I matter?

For those who wonder if you are supposed to be alive, who think you might be an accident, who believe you exist because of a cosmic glitch—let me assure you: you are alive for a reason. No, you are *not* an accident. And cosmic glitches, real or imagined, have nothing to do with your conception and birth.

Maybe you need this message to ring in your ears: "You were created on purpose with purpose to fulfill a purpose." Any questions about your identity are not your fault. Period.

Want to know what your Creator says about your existence? The Bible speaks to God's intent when He made you and His plan for your life. Look up the following scriptures and make them personal; where applicable insert your name, because God means them personally about you: Genesis 1:27; Joshua 1:9; Psalms 100:3; 139:13–16; Jeremiah 1:5; 29:11; Ephesians 2:10; and Colossians 1:16.

Why do I know so much about this subject?

At age forty-six, through a series of dramatic events, I discovered my dad is not my biological father. He didn't know. My mom didn't either.

Now, before you come unglued at my last statement, let me say that my mother was aware of the possibility—a slight chance I was conceived through a one-time interaction with another man—someone she knew, but not someone with whom she pursued a sexual encounter. Out of respect for her and my biological father, I'll leave it at that.

As a public speaker drawn to help the hurting, I meet many people in similar situations as my own. Reactions to identity issues vary among the men and women I meet, often depending on how a person learned the truth of his or her heritage. If children are raised knowing they are family by choice, versus by blood, their trauma lessens, as do their symptoms.

For those who are rocked by surprising news, it can feel as if their lives are built on half-truths—the rugs of all they believed about their existence are ripped from underneath them.

When this happens, there is some sort of fallout—whether docile or dramatic, seething or screaming. Outbursts of rage, withdrawal from everyday activities, black depressive states, inability to sleep, strange dreams or nightmares, eating disorders, substance abuse, and more can indicate post-traumatic stress from unanswered questions to how our lives began. If we don't recognize the root cause, we waste years trying to repress our pain.

And the number of people experiencing these issues is growing, in particular because of absent fathers. Too many men are referred to as sperm donors, baby daddies, or bio fathers. But for the child, this is not enough—even when we try to convince ourselves and others that it's no big deal. We define ourselves intrinsically through our fathers and mothers.

From the time we are very small children, we need to know Daddy will keep us safe from the boogeyman and big monsters. The frightened little girl or boy inside of us wants to know our father will snatch us away from danger before we are harmed.

But when fathers can't or don't protect us from life's hurts, a crust develops around our tender, bruised hearts. If Daddy leaves, whether we remember the event or not, our worst fears are realized. Abandonment.

We can spend the rest of our lives trying to prevent

it from happening again. Trying to regain control of the uncontrollable. As we do, the crust around our heart thickens, running wider and deeper—crushing the soft places and making us hard as flint.

Grown women will carry a scared little girl inside them wherever they go. A woman who sustains parental loss or perceives rejection from childhood lives in terror of experiencing it as an adult. She desperately tries to prevent it, and she often chases love and acceptance down dangerous alleys.

Grown men will carry a wounded little boy inside them. They strive to protect themselves by hurting others first, before someone has the chance to strike them. Their mission is defense.

In each case, gender doesn't always define reaction. Sometimes response roles reverse. But no matter how women and men conduct themselves outwardly, without learning the mastery of how to get through it they can spend a lifetime trying to get over the missing pieces of their origin.

Identity seekers throw many ineffective things into a dark cavity, when there is a healthy way to fill the void of a missing parent. Angela's story below, a compilation based on real people, shows us how to deal with our biological concerns in a healthy way. She discovered the enigma of a Father without physical arms, who hugs tightly, who never leaves, never abandons, and always loves. Through the dark valley of identity questions, she sought and found hope when she was introduced to her real Daddy.

The woman's hands spoke with her questions as she took a couple of steps toward the right side of the stage. "The truth will set you free. Have you heard it? Do you believe it?" Her short dark hair accented a friendly face, long with high cheekbones. Her green eyes sparkled with energy.

"Do you know what it's like to have a secret so big that the thought of telling it makes your heart feel like it will burst through your chest? You break into a cold sweat when you imagine other people finding out? Does it make you afraid you might lose everything important to you?" She moved to her left, scanning the entire audience with her eyes. "We all do things we wish we could take back. Everyone has something they wanted to conceal from the world, and often from themselves. No one wants these deeds pulled out of the dark corners of unspoken sin and displayed. We hope we can hide them forever."

The woman's insightful scrutiny made Angela shift in her seat. A friend had invited her to this luncheon, but she had no idea the message would be directed at her.

"There's a category of secret that changes everything if revealed. The keeper of the mystery believes telling will destroy relationships, break hearts, ruin lives. They fear ripping away the core values of everyone affected if the truth is exposed."

The intensity etched on the Stonecroft speaker's face transformed to a softer, compassionate expression. "My story is about a woman who held such a secret for almost fifty years—my mom. And her secret involved me."

Angela straightened her posture. Where was this going?

"I've known since I was twelve that my parents wed because of me, and as a child I felt emotional weight because of it. But I didn't know there was more to the story."

The woman had Angela's full attention now.

"When I was forty-eight, I found out my dad wasn't my birth father, and I was the result of my mom's affair with a married man. When I discovered how I was truly conceived, it was a shock."

A sadness crept into the woman's features. "My parents divorced when I was sixteen. I remembered their years of fighting and making up and wondered if they felt trapped into getting married. Was I the source of their misery? Was their unhappiness my fault?"

Angela felt the rest of the room melt into the background, as if the speaker were carrying on an intimate conversation with her.

The woman continued, "I rebelled, running harder and faster toward anything that represented love. I built a wall of protection around my heart. I slipped into the slimy pit of depression. I couldn't pull myself up by the bootstraps. I wasn't capable of snapping out of it. Thinking happy thoughts didn't work—I couldn't remember any."

She leaned closer toward the audience. "No one wants to feel bad. You don't get depressed for attention.

Anxiety attacks are not a welcome friend. In reality, negative emotions are enemies of a peace-filled, whole life."

Angela knew far too much about those statements.

"During this time, out of desperation, I picked up a Bible, and God inched me toward His healing light. It was a slow process. Sometimes I couldn't read and only had the strength to hold the Bible to my chest while I scrunched into a fetal position. But over weeks and months, I eventually discovered encouragement through its motivational stories and energizing scriptures. I found a cure on those pages."

Skepticism crept into Angela's thoughts.

"Glimmers of hope lifted my spirits when I read Joshua 1:9, 'Be strong and courageous. Do not be afraid; do not be discouraged, for the LORD your God will be with you wherever you go.' " She lifted up a thick book with worn corners. "My tears stained the page when He told me through Jeremiah 1:5, 'Before I formed you in the womb I knew you, before you were born *I set you apart*.' " She dropped the Bible on the podium and said in a softer tone, "I needed to know God's promise from Psalm 68:5, that He would be 'a father to the fatherless.' "

Angela picked up her glass of water, hoping the drink masked the salty drops trickling down her face. She then pretended to dab her mouth with a napkin, discreetly allowing the fabric to brush higher, drying wet cheeks. Angela couldn't comprehend how this woman could speak so openly about her secret. But it felt oddly comforting, so Angela focused her attention back on the story.

"As I read more, I recognized myself as a wounded little girl who needed a Father. And I found Him. God is my Daddy. Instead of running away from Him, I ran straight into His arms and let Him pick me up and soothe my hurts."

The woman closed her eyes, and a slight smile broadened her cheeks. "I imagined crawling up into my Daddy's lap. I pictured Him brushing my hair from my eyes, stroking my cheek, kissing the tip of my nose and chin while he wiped the tears from my face. I lay my head on His chest and felt His heart beat for me. Have you ever done that when you hurt? Did you know you can?"

Angela gulped.

"I opened my Bible, begging God to say something special. It flipped open to John 15:3, and I was amazed when I read, 'You are already clean because of the word I have spoken to you.'

"He was telling me I wasn't dirty, something few people knew I struggled with due to the way I was conceived. But God's confirmation was personal, and it let me know I wasn't alone in this journey."

Angela eyed the thick chunk of chocolate cake set before her. She had resolved earlier not to indulge. Now she poured a cup of coffee from the carafe and sliced her fork into the piece of gooey comfort. But still, her ears were listening.

"A dear friend said this in response to my story:

'God sure went through a lot of trouble to create you. He must have a special plan for your life.' "

Angela laid down the fork.

The woman's passion heightened. "I've learned she is right. I am not an accident. God knitted me together on purpose with purpose to fulfill a purpose. My unique DNA combination makes me especially qualified to do the work He planned for me before I was even born. I *am* wanted, because my Daddy God is my Father. I *am* the daughter of the King of kings, which makes me a princess. I *am* secure in my identity, which is found in Christ alone. I *am* beautiful, because I look like my Daddy in heaven."

Angela glanced at her friend, who smiled and winked, oblivious to the turmoil brewing beneath the nod Angela returned.

The woman stepped closer to the edge of the stage and in a hushed tone said, "The truth has set me free. It set my mom free in so many ways. The release of this secret has lifted a heavy burden off our lives. It was an invisible prison, keeping us bound."

Angela held her breath.

"I urge you, if you're keeping a secret, don't let it hold you prisoner. If your personal identity is in question, don't let it define you. You have a loving Daddy, no matter how you were conceived or raised. Just say yes to His call for your attention. Your Daddy wants a relationship with you. Know you are loved and wanted—you don't have to walk this journey alone. You are not forsaken or abandoned. Your Daddy is waiting with arms open wide."

And then it was over. The crowd stood to their feet, applauding and cheering. Angela stood as well, clapping quietly, stunned at what she had just heard.

When she left, Angela drove to a quiet park instead of going home. She pulled her car to a stop under the shade of a large sycamore tree and rolled the window down, allowing the soft breezes of a flawless spring day to wash over her. The scent of honeysuckle calmed her throbbing nerves. She knew it was time.

Angela tilted her head back, touching the headrest behind her. Then with a deep breath of courage, she opened a mental door she'd kept locked for twenty-two years.

She was fourteen when she found out. The day of Daddy's funeral. Nibbling on a tasteless cracker with cheese when Aunt Pamela, Daddy's sister, walked up and hugged her tight. A few thoughtless words spoken through a veil of grief turned Angela's life upside down.

Aunt Pamela stroked Angela's hair while she spoke. "He loved you as if you were his own."

Angela stiffened instantly.

The body language signaled Pamela, revealing the mistake she'd just made. She pulled back from her embrace, blotches of red dotting her neck and face, her gushes of apology worsening the situation. "Oh honey, I am so sorry. Please forgive me. I swore I'd never tell you."

Needing a momentary break from the memory, Angela lifted a bottle of Diet Dr Pepper to her lips and pulled on the cool, bubbling liquid. The sweet flavor mixed with the burn on her throat felt good, strengthening her resolve to visit a time she'd hoped to forget.

After ripping open the can of confusion, Aunt Pamela didn't offer details. She dismissed herself, practically running out of the room. A few minutes later, Angela saw her aunt whispering to her mom, arms flailing while she talked.

Her mom's lips had tightened, but she didn't open them to speak. From Angela's perspective, it looked as if there was little to say.

Questions riddling her mind, Angela walked toward the two older women, ready to find out why her aunt would say such strange things. But she was cut off by a man from their church offering his condolences. By the time Angela was able to move on, Aunt Pamela had left the house and a circle of well-wishers had surrounded her mother.

Exasperated, Angela slid away to take cover in her room.

From her bedroom window, Angela watched the last of the mourners leave. She wasted no time going downstairs to find her mother on the couch, rubbing circles over her temples.

Angela's emotions seemed to swirl into each other. She felt a mix of sympathy and anger toward her mother, while fearing what she would hear next. But she was still compelled to ask. "Why would Aunt Pamela say Dad loved me like his own?"

Her mom's eyes were swollen slits. "I always meant to tell you. But your dad—he didn't want to confuse you when you were little. Neither did I. You've grown up so fast, fourteen already. I guess time slipped away from us. When your dad got cancer, we decided to wait until after he beat it." Her mom dropped her face into the palms of her hands and spoke through the fingered mask. "But he didn't beat it. Cancer took him from us."

Angela could feel tentacles of anxiety constrict her throat. "What are you saying? Dad's my father? Right?"

Her mother pulled tear-soaked hands from her face. "Not biologically. But he is your dad, and you are his only child. We found out a few years after we married that he couldn't produce children."

Angela shook her head, as if to rattle reality back in place. This was crazy. Then the obvious question blurted its way out of her mouth. "Who *is* my father?"

"I don't know."

Images immediately played across Angela's mind. A younger version of her mother, head back, laughing, flirting, standing in a circle of young men all vying for her attention. Was one of those unknown faces her father?

But that image didn't match what Angela knew of her mother's personality. Her character. Her nature. Now she wondered, did she really know her mother at all?

Angela felt her eyes narrow involuntarily. "How can you not know who my father is? You're the only one who does know. Why won't you tell me? If there's more than one possibility, give me their names and I'll find out myself. I read an article the other day that said you can get paternity DNA tests at most drugstores now."

Her mom flinched. "Are you sure you want to know the truth?"

"I can handle it."

Her mother sighed. "When I was twenty-four, I was walking home from work." She pursed her mouth. "If only I'd let my friend give me a ride when she offered."

Angela held her breath.

"I was standing in front of this pale yellow house, the kind with a white fence and brightly colored flowers planted perfectly around a neatly kept yard. An orange tree bent near the roofline, and the flowers let off a heavy perfume. I still hate the smell of orange blossoms. Anyway, I heard a bird singing above my head, and I craned my neck to see what kind it was. I had to shield my eyes from the sun to look up. Then a man startled me, asking for my help.

"I looked down, and there was this guy, probably in his early thirties, clean-cut, looked nice enough. I asked him naively, 'With what?'

" 'I need to move a bag of potting soil in my shed, but I pulled my back the other day, and I can't move it by myself. Would you mind?'

"I told him, 'Of course not,' then walked through his gate and followed him to the shed.

"It was dark inside and smelled musty. I knew something was wrong when he pulled the door shut behind me. It happened so fast. He threw me on the bags of potting soil and clamped his hand over my mouth. One of his fingers almost touched my nose, making it hard to breathe. I thought I was going to suffocate. For a while, time seemed to stop. I feared being stuck in that hell forever. But finally it ended.

"He rolled off me and growled, 'Get out of here. And you'd better not say a word to anyone about this. I know where to find you.'

"Terrified, I kept the secret. I met your dad two days later. I didn't know I was already pregnant with you. He was gentle and kind. At first he didn't understand why I pulled away when he touched my arm or why I stiffened when he put his arm around my waist, but he was patient while he waited for me to trust him. And eventually I did.

"Enough to tell him what happened to me when I found out I was pregnant.

"By then he'd already told me he loved me. But the moment he found out about you, he was determined to marry me. At first I said no, but he was relentless." Angela's mom chuckled. "I couldn't refuse him. And I've never regretted that decision. Your dad was the best thing that ever happened to me. To us."

Sitting in her car, adult Angela remembered the sting—the night she found out her whole life was built on a lie.

After the initial revelation, on numerous occasions Angela's mother offered to talk more, but Angela refused. What was the point? It wasn't like she was going to find her father—or wanted to.

So Angela went on with her life, pretending she'd never found out the ugly truth of her conception. Convincing herself she didn't care, though the proof was written on her frame. Years of stuffing food over unsettled emotions had added pounds to her figure.

But she could avoid it no more. Hearing the speaker today, knowing there were others with similar identity issues out there, made the illusion melt away, bringing her to confront God and herself in a park on a sunny spring day.

Angela soon sought a therapist. It took months of counseling, many self-discovery exercises, and opening herself up to talk about her situation, but over time Angela learned to accept. She made a list of things she could not control and faced what she could control with determination.

She also picked up a Bible, reading it for the first time. There she met her Father in its ancient text, the One she now calls her real Daddy. Learning to love and accept herself, knowing God's effort made her just the way she is, purposed as a daughter of the King of kings.

Being created or raised in less than ideal circumstances plays on your mind. Whether it's a paternity question or residual abandonment issues trailing into your adult years, these things don't go away.

This requires treatment on many fronts. Even with professional guidance, you must realize no one else can do this work for you. You must shift from allowing your subconscious to define you and resolve to move through a situation you cannot change. However, you don't have to do it alone. You have a Father who will carry you through.

The two greatest commandments as told by Christ in Mark 12:30–31 are "Love the Lord your God with all your heart and with all your soul and with all your mind and with all your strength" and "Love your neighbor as yourself." But the last part can get sticky: "Love. . .yourself." Folks with identity problems often struggle with self-love.

Notice that "love" is a verb in these verses, not a warm and fuzzy noun. It is an intentional choice we act on. Give yourself permission to love God, neighbors, and yourself in emotional, spiritual, mental, and physical ways. These demonstrate acceptance in action. It's okay for you to be alive, and it's okay to live like you believe that. This is the message your loving Father wants you to internalize—it will free you from imprisonment by lies.

Another PTSD prison is smothering debt. Next we'll learn how to unlock self-made cells. Do you feel trapped? If so, find release in the following pages. The Master says, "Your term is up."

INSIDER INSIGHTS

Emotional Healing

- Music soothes the hurting heart. Natalie Grant's "Held" is a beautiful reminder that regardless of conception, you have a Daddy who loves you unconditionally. He will never deny you time and attention.

- Find something that symbolizes your true identity as a child of the King of kings—a necklace, ring, or something you carry in your wallet or purse. Let your symbol be a reminder, not something you worship. Make it personal between you and the One who made you—on purpose with purpose to fulfill a purpose.
- Write notes to Daddy. Use a daily or weekly journal to pour out your heart to the Perfect Parent who is never too tired, self-absorbed, or overwhelmed to listen to your feelings.

Practical Help

- Choose one positive trait about yourself, and celebrate your unique difference. God went to a lot of trouble to make you, and you are worth commemorating.
- Post notes to remind yourself, "I am supposed to be alive. I am loved."
- Become aware if you are self-medicating with food and/or drink, shopping, sex, or any other substitute for acceptance. Substance abuse comes in many forms besides alcohol and drugs. When you crave something to fill the void, take a one-minute interval where you jog in place, do jumping jacks, or some other vigorous physical activity before stuffing morsels in your mouth—or doing anything else you might regret.

Spiritual Comfort

- You are not an accident, a mistake, or a cosmic glitch. Much intentionality went into making you exactly who you are. If God says you are marvelously made, who are you to argue (see Psalm 139:13–16)?

- Don't let an unchosen past define you or make you a fearful slave. It's not your fault. Instead, receive God's Spirit, who comes into your life when God adopts you as His own child. Then you can call God "Abba, Father," a Daddy who loves you apart from conditions (see Romans 8:15).

- We all need an advocate. The Father to the fatherless and defender of the widow is your Daddy. He's got your back, and He will never abandon you (see Psalm 68:5).

GUIDED PRAYER

Dear Daddy,

Thank You for letting me crawl into Your lap. Thank You for brushing wisps of hair off my forehead, for stroking my cheek, kissing the tip of my nose and the bottom of my chin. Thank You for letting me lay my head on Your chest and rest, knowing, no matter what, You will never leave.

CHAPTER 4

Debt and Daddy's Hands

P aid in full."

Who wouldn't like to hear those words or see them stamped on a financial document? The fact is, however, thousands of people around the globe are living in modern-day debtor's prison. According to CreditCards.com, global indebtedness has escalated to a level unmatched in previous history.

Overleveraged accounts consume more than our finances; they also consume our minds and emotions. We are smothered by stress when our outstanding bills grow at a faster rate than our income. Innumerable people struggle, trying not to drown in the monthly bills flooding in.

With an influx of instant credit offers, as well as looming bills, many women and men are tempted to jump at quick fixes, such as acquiring payday loans, borrowing from friends or family, or shifting money from high-interest cards to credit lines offering zero percent or a low interest rate through balance transfers. Sometimes they do this without their mate's knowledge.

Hoping to keep the peace through their secret debt exchanges, the offending spouse unknowingly makes matters worse, especially if the origin of the deception is grounded in issues unrelated to finances. Money difficulties are symptoms, usually related to deep-seated PTSD, and are not root problems. These tough financial situations are born from a past that men and women have worked hard to bury.

Recently one woman told me her story, and though it was the first time I'd spoken to her, it wasn't the first time I'd heard this type of tale. I've changed her name and used details from other narratives to protect her privacy, as well as speeded up the timeline. But Sherri is a real person, and from the interviews I've done, there are many out there like her—maybe someone like you or someone you know who struggles under the weight of growing bills.

If she was right in her estimates, it would be here today. Sherri nervously opened the mailbox, shuffling through white envelopes. The red lettering in the return address corner caught her eye. Sure enough, the credit card statement had arrived—and she had safely snatched it before her husband got home.

Sherri folded the envelope into a tight square and shoved it into her back pocket, then tossed the remaining parcels back into the mailbox. She'd only taken a couple of steps when her cell rang. It was Levi. Sherri's heart quickened, so she breathed deeply, letting the scent of fresh-cut grass pacify her before answering. "Hey, babe."

"What are you doing?"

Feeling guilt whitewash her stomach with sour fear, Sherri fibbed. "Taking a walk on my lunch hour."

"You'll need a shower before you go back to work."

Focused on keeping the tremor out of her voice, Sherri tried to sound nonchalant. "I'm just taking a short one."

Her husband changed the subject. "Rick asked me to go to the lake this weekend."

"Again?"

"What do you mean 'again'? It's been almost a month since the last time."

"But it's expensive. Almost five hundred dollars every time you go." Sherri heard the whine in her voice and tried to soften it. "The house insurance is due in a couple of weeks, and we need to make sure it's covered."

"Are you telling me I can't afford to go to the lake?"

Sherri heard the implied threat beneath the question. She reacted swiftly. "Forget it."

"I've told you I hate those four words. Don't tell me 'We can't afford it.' "

"I'll take care of it."

"How?"

"I've got some money put back." Sherri's stomach clenched at the lie she told.

"I knew you were holding out."

"Yeah—holding out."

Satisfied, Levi maneuvered the conversation again. "I'll be a little late tonight. Gotta pay my gym membership so I can keep myself in the shape you're accustomed to." He laughed at his own joke.

The sound of Levi's chuckling echoed in Sherri's ear; then the line went dead.

Sherri opened her car door and dropped behind

the wheel. The searing smell of broiling upholstery gave her an instant headache, while heat from the leather seat singed her leg where her skirt had bunched up. She yelped and bounced like a cat on a trampoline, bumping her knee in the process. In seconds, her whole face was slathered in sweat. Sherri started the car, hoping the air conditioner would cause the sweltering smells and temperature to dissipate. But she knew the heat wasn't what was really bothering her. If only she had a button to make their debt go away.

When Sherri returned from lunch, she settled into her duties as a receptionist for Dr. John Marks. Patients were already crammed in the waiting area, with two new ones filling out paperwork. She marked names off the list, chatting with her coworker at the same time.

"Shoot."

"What's wrong?" Patty stepped closer.

"I scrubbed a name I shouldn't have. Mr. Larson hasn't seen the doctor yet."

"Oh, that's all. A silly mistake."

"But I'm making more of them lately. I don't know what's wrong with me. I'm not sleeping well. At least three times in the past month I woke up feeling like a rhino was sitting on my chest. My appetite is off, and my body's not functioning properly." Sherri rolled her chair backward and whispered, "I had Dr. Marks run some tests. They all came back normal, but my body's totally out of control and I don't know why."

"He didn't have any suggestions?"

"He said I'm probably having anxiety attacks. He

wants to refer me to a counselor."

"What did Levi say?"

"I haven't told him. Money's tight. Besides, he'll tell me to do whatever I need to, but what he really means is, as long as he can do what he wants."

"That's tough. I've never had an anxiety attack, but another friend of mine has, and they sound horrible. She says almost anything can launch one. It's really strange. She was in a car accident last year, and even though she only sustained minor injuries, she's battled anxiety ever since."

Sherri crinkled her eyebrows. "I haven't experienced a traumatic event. Unless you count trying to keep up with Levi's spending. Don't get me wrong; he's not extravagant, but a little here and a little there adds up. He expects me to magically make money appear. If I say anything, he gets mad, like it's all my fault."

"I wouldn't put up with it."

"Levi's good to me. He works hard, he comes home every night, and he doesn't hit me."

"Isn't that what husbands are supposed to do?"

"My dad didn't."

Patty laid a gentle hand on Sherri's shoulder. "Maybe you should let Dr. Marks give you that referral."

"I guess I'd better get back to work." Sherri moved her chair toward the desk.

The thought of telling someone else her private business made Sherri feel queasy. Even Levi didn't know the extent of her childhood. She couldn't think about it right now, so she pushed old memories back where they belonged.

When Sherri arrived home that evening, she plopped her purse on the counter. Opening the refrigerator and then the freezer, she groaned, speaking to the empty room. "I don't feel like cooking tonight. My head hurts, and I'm not hungry." But she couldn't entertain the option of not fixing dinner. They didn't have the funds to eat out. So Sherri scoured the cabinets and looked deeper in the fridge until she came up with ingredients to make a decent meal.

She poured herself a glass of sweet tea and sipped while she forced herself to cook. Nearly an hour later, the aroma roused Sherri's appetite. Now she was ready to eat.

True to his word, Levi was late, but much later than Sherri expected. How long could it take to renew a gym membership anyway? Sherri had texted three times, with no response. He finally breezed in the door a few minutes before eight.

"Where have you been? Our supper's cold."

"Sorry, babe, after the gym I ran by the mall to get a new case for my iPhone."

"What's wrong with your old one?"

"Nothing. I'm giving it to Chris. But I wanted a LifeProof. It protects your phone from water damage up to six submerged meters."

"You don't scuba dive—or even swim, for that matter. Why would you need a case to protect your phone from submersion?"

"Lots of reasons. I could drop it in the sink. In the bathtub. Or in the toilet."

Sherri shook her head in disbelief. "How much did this set us back?"

"They had a sale. It was only forty bucks, marked down 20 percent. Besides, I'm a grown man. I work for a living. Don't tell me I can't spend my own money."

Levi's challenge caused the familiar fear to creep up Sherri's spine. Her gut spasmed. "Let's just eat, okay?"

"I picked up a burger and fries on the way home. Sorry. What'd you fix?"

Sherri marched to the kitchen without answering, slamming dishes and cabinet doors. She looked at the food she had cooked, congealed remnants of an hour's worth of her time. Remembering her exhaustion while standing over the stove, she scraped the entire meal into the trash bin.

As soon as she straightened, it hit. A full-blown panic attack. Starting deep in the bowel of her lower belly, a fiery trail of adrenaline spread toward her heart. A low burn increased the pumping in her organs, pulsing faster beats of air and blood.

Then the sensation of a single blow to her chest, followed by thousands of needles poking her simultaneously from the inside. She doubled over, hoping to move pressure from whatever pushed against her flaming lungs. She gasped for oxygen. She felt like she might spontaneously combust.

The entire episode only lasted four minutes, although it felt like four hours to Sherri. Yet Levi didn't have a clue. He hadn't followed her when she left the room. He never did. As always, Sherri kept her escalating struggles to herself, praying desperately for answers to her problems. She dealt with it alone.

Levi was asleep when Sherri slid under the sheets. She scowled at him, resenting his ability to rest peacefully. She hoped her own fatigue would counter the agitation she felt. Sherry was desperate for a good night's slumber.

The room was black with a green glow from the alarm clock when Sherri bolted upright in the middle of the night. A new round of panic causing her to hyperventilate. She looked toward her nightstand—2:14 a.m.

Sherri pushed on various locations around her abdomen with her fingers, hoping to prod a gas bubble, forcing it to burst and let her breathe freely. She bent her knees and dropped her face between them—maybe breathing through the comforter would calm her screaming lungs.

It took awhile for her body to respond to her slow, methodical breaths. But finally, Sherri felt settled enough to stretch her legs flat. She looked at the clock again: 3:58 a.m. Sherri counted on her fingers. She'd lost almost an hour and forty-five minutes, time she could never get back. This had to stop.

The next morning, Levi pecked Sherri warily on the cheek as he left for work. A sheepish "Love you" was his only comment.

She knew he felt bad; Levi was a decent man. Sherri knew she should stand up to him instead of shutting down. If she'd had more courage early in their marriage, odds were they wouldn't be in the shape they were in now.

A sharp pang of fear stung her as an old thought invaded. *Dad*.

She suddenly remembered a dream she'd had last night. Levi had bought a new boat—actually it was a yacht. They were floating lazily through a sun-washed channel when money started blowing in the air all around them.

Levi started chasing it while Sherri screamed, "No. Don't."

She reached out to stop him; then suddenly he fell overboard, and she lost sight of him in a hurricane of one-hundred-dollar bills. A few seconds later, he reappeared, but he wasn't himself. His face, a mixture of his own and her father's, distorted in anger. He swung a heavy club. And he was swinging at her.

Sherri's stomach tensed. Was this what woke her up in the middle of an anxiety attack last night? Where were these weird ideas coming from? Did her dream have some kind of meaning?

Sherri made a decision. She would talk to Dr. Marks about counseling options today. Money or no money, she needed answers.

Three days later, Sherri walked up to the sliding glass window. A discreet sign read LAUREN HARLAN, LPC. A dark-haired woman wearing a sweet smile slid the partition back and said, "Can I help you?"

"I have an appointment with the doctor."

"Certainly. Have you seen her before?"

"No."

"Great. Welcome to our office. And I should clarify, Lauren's a licensed professional counselor, not a doctor, although I sometimes call her a miracle worker." The woman's light laughter tinkled through the inviting room decorated with soft pillows in soothing tones of sky blue and golden yellow. "I'm going to give you some paperwork to fill out, but if you have any questions, come back and see me. I'm happy to help."

It didn't escape Sherri's notice that the woman's demeanor on the job was vastly different from her own. In their short exchange, Sherri recognized how much she'd allowed her personal worries to influence the way she treated Dr. Marks's patients. She scolded herself and determined to change her work attitude immediately.

Soon Lauren, as she told Sherri to call her, took back for their first session. The counselor kept things light and informal, asking periodic questions about background, but it didn't feel intimidating—rather like new friends getting to know each other.

Similar to the lobby, Lauren's office felt welcoming and warm, although the colors were different. Mellow greens, white, and muted touches of red infused the room. Shortly into their conversation, Lauren pointed to a Keurig coffeemaker sitting on a small table with a large lace doily beneath it. "Would you like a cup of coffee or tea?"

Once Sherri held the steaming tea, she could tell they were going to broach deeper subjects. A twinge of unease squeezed her stomach.

"Do you want to talk about what brings you here today?"

Sherri was surprised to feel her eyes well up. She started with their financial difficulties and ended up telling all the fine details, things she'd never spoken out loud to anyone else. "I opened a credit card without Levi's knowledge. Not because I'm a big shopper—I hardly spend anything on myself—except when I get mad at him for wasting money. Then I do justify a few minor purchases."

Lauren nodded compassionately.

Sherri expected condemnation, in words or expression, but Lauren delivered neither. So Sherri continued. "I forged his name on the application. We've got decent credit because we pay our bills on time, but barely. I'm afraid it's catching up with us. I had to take out a cash advance to pay our house insurance because Levi's going to the lake again. When I hinted we couldn't afford it, he got mad. So I backed down."

"What does it look like when he gets mad at you? Describe the scene."

Sherri drew a verbal picture of the fight she and Levi had a few days back. Telling Lauren it was more than her husband's trip to the lake, but the small expenditures like his phone case and eating out that added to their bills—causing her stress to escalate.

When Sherri finished, Lauren said, "Close your eyes, and imagine you are telling Levi about the secret credit card. You're explaining to him how hard it is for you to keep up with his everyday spending. Picture his face, allow yourself to hear his tone of voice, envision his body language. Now explain what you see."

Sherri's breath stopped midway up her throat. She was shocked. In no time, an angry Levi transformed into her father. And a dark memory from her childhood came crashing out of the box she'd locked it in. A raging panic attack followed right behind.

Lauren guided Sherri with soothing kindness. "Let yourself feel it, but don't forget, you are safe. Tell me what you see."

"I'm little. Maybe two or three. Daddy's driving. I'm buckled in my car seat, and I can see the dark hair on the back of his head."

"Go on."

"Our old car smells of grease and oil, Daddy's smell. He was a workingman, always fixing things. At first I feel protected. Safe. I look out the window as we pull off the highway onto a long driveway, nestled down a dirt country lane."

"Do you know where you're going?"

"I see Grandpa and Grandma's house. Mommy laughs at something he says, and I join in. My voice tinkles, and I like the feeling in my throat. Daddy's shoulders shake in a pleasant sort of way. He starts to tease me, asking me to repeat what he says, 'My name is Sherri Edwards, and I'm mean as a snake.'"

"Did you say it?"

"Sure. Over and over, in my toddler voice I say, 'My name is Shewi Edwards, and I'm mean as a 'nake.' He makes fun of me because I can't pronounce my r's and s's properly. But it's okay, because he's laughing. So I laugh at myself. I feel so good. I have Daddy's full attention.

And he's happy with me."

"Was it unusual for him to be happy with you?"

"I really can't say. This is the first thing I remember about my life."

"So this is your first memory?"

"Yes. I don't know why we were going to my grandparents, but I was so excited. When my daddy carried me into the kitchen, my breath caught. I'd never seen anything like it. It was tall and elegant. White, silver, with rich purple flowers. Where it sat on the counter, the sun shone on it with a golden spotlight. But the two pieces sparkling on the top mesmerized me the most. Grandma took me out of Daddy's arms.

"She kissed my cheek and said, 'Do you want to see?'

"I didn't speak—I couldn't. The glittering bride and groom were magical."

Lauren spoke reverently, as if she understood Sherri's enchantment with the memory. "It was a wedding cake?"

"Yes. Grandma carried me to the kitchen table, still mussed with splatters of flour. She moved a paper bag, and I saw them. Another bride and groom pair.

" 'Would you like to hold them?' Grandma picked up the edible cake toppers.

"My chunky little fingers clambered for the sugary confections. I caressed my cheek with the strange sensation of scratchy sweetness. I'd never felt anything so exquisite, and I clutched them as if they were a priceless treasure.

"I don't know how long we stayed, but when Daddy

said, 'It's time to go home,' I was scared I'd have to give my little bride and groom back. But Grandma said I could keep them.

"I clutched the sugary newlyweds in my tiny hands, glancing at their delicate sparkles in the sunlight as we walked to the car.

" 'What have you got?' Daddy grabbed my wrist and twisted it so my palm pointed up, exposing my sweet, sugar-spun couple.

"My grandmother stepped in before I could answer. 'I gave them to her.'

"He dropped my hand. 'You'd better not make a mess in the car.' Daddy buckled me in my seat. Then he backed the car and turned us around. We headed up the winding dirt driveway.

"We had just arrived home when it happened.

"Daddy opened the door to get me out. I touched his shoulder.

"His scream reverberated across the back seat of our small car. 'Get that sticky mess off of me!'

"I started wailing instantly. I knew the venom in his voice meant danger.

" 'Stop your crying, or I'll give you something to cry about.'

"His threat had the opposite effect. The pitch in my sobs increased, bouncing off the rolled-up windows and boomeranging to hurt my own ears.

"Daddy ground the next words through gritted teeth more than speaking them to me. 'If you don't stop, I'll throw that piece of junk away.'

"I tried to stop; I really did. But my hiccups and

sniffling did little to ebb the tears. I grasped the bride and groom tight to my little chest as if to protect them. 'O–o–okay, Da–Daddy.'

"When he picked me up, I must have brushed his neck, because he started swiping at it while he screeched at me. I remember the look in his eyes—they seemed to turn black. I could smell coffee on his breath when he said, 'I told you.'

"He unfurled my balled fist and snatched my treasures away. Then he flung them onto our driveway. The head of the sugar-spun groom snapped off, bouncing toward our mailbox. The bride shattered, her body splattered in a mass of white sparkles beside the car.

"I twisted, trying to get out of Daddy's arms so I could scoop up what was left.

"My ear rang before I felt the sting. It jarred my face so hard, I felt my teeth shake. My breath sucked into my lungs at the precise moment of impact, holding momentarily until I released it in a howl. In that moment, something changed inside my soul. I felt so betrayed. After that, the rest of the day is a blur."

The air in Lauren's office echoed with silence. Neither client nor counselor spoke for several minutes. Finally, Lauren broke the quiet.

"How have you dealt with your abuse?"

"What do you mean?"

"I assume your father's outburst wasn't a one-time incident."

"He didn't hit me every day. And mostly I deserved it when he did."

Lauren grimaced and lowered her head. "Did your mother help?"

"She did what she could, but Dad was harder on her than on me. Dad wasn't really abusive; he was more of a strict disciplinarian."

A bell chimed, signaling the end of their session. Lauren made a new appointment before Sherri left.

Through subsequent meetings, Sherri learned how ingrained her childhood trauma was in her psyche and how much it affected the way she responded, especially to Levi. She hadn't realized the pain she'd buried from her past was bubbling up to hurt her in the present.

Once she did, Sherri took a courageous step and sat Levi down, revealing things about herself she'd hidden. About her father and how she feared her husband would react with similar violence if things weren't perfect. About the measures she took to keep him happy so he wouldn't get mad at her.

Eventually, Sherri mustered the courage to discuss finances with her husband. Levi didn't react well to the truth about their debt initially, but he didn't leave either.

With Lauren's support, along with prayers from a women's mentoring group, Sherri stopped cowering in fear. And she also experienced a surprise side effect of a positive nature.

After years of battling weight problems, Sherri learned how to apply the principles that had helped her take courage with her husband to healthier lifestyle habits. In less than a year's time, a svelte, smiling Sherri had less debt and more confidence. Before and after, her exterior reflected her response to childhood abuse, something she would never get over. But Sherri was getting through.

According to national statistics, every ten seconds a report of child abuse is made. Surviving children grow into adults, many exhibiting mild to moderate symptoms of PTSD.

The best remedy is to prevent abuse, but when it's too late and injuries have occurred, many boys and girls attempt to bury emotions with the memories. They medicate their way into adulthood, shoveling things over pulsing wounds, hiding anything that might cause trouble, learning to avoid honest communication.

For some, the seed of financial symptoms does not originate in childhood abuse. Other factors are at work.

After researching numerous psychology articles by experts in the field, a trend emerged in what I discovered. Overspending or hoarding, whether by regular habit or in binges, derives from attempts to avoid painful emotions, medicate depression, mask low self-esteem, or fulfill an intrinsic need for instant gratification.

But whatever is at its core, the first step in overcoming unhealthy finances is to create an action plan: Address. Assess. Confess. Progress.

Address the reasons why you spend. Honestly *assess* what you've spent up until now. *Confess* your expenditures to God—there is no debt your Daddy can't help you pay in full. And *progress* with a mission and goal to reduce what you owe. If you are married, each of these steps requires the participation of your spouse. Remember what Proverbs 28:13 says: "Whoever conceals their sins does not prosper, but the one who confesses and renounces them finds mercy."

When spending is our go-to, we constantly worry about where the money is going to come from versus why we're spending to begin with. If people-pleasing is our vice, we try harder instead of questioning what we're trying to appease.

But I believe we were created for more. More freedom. More satisfaction. More joy.

Only by facing our past will healing occur from the true source of our problematic habits today. By partnering our efforts with God's plan for abundant living, we can unlock the door on any modern-day debtor's prison.

Invest time, a teachable spirit, consistency, and belief in an outcome you cannot yet see. With practiced faith set to work, it is possible to restore your finances and, as we'll discuss next, find relief from your chronic worries.

Insider Insights

Emotional Healing

- "Whom Shall I Fear" by Chris Tomlin is our watch song for this chapter. Let its healing balm bind your wounds.

- Work on honesty exercises. First with yourself. Practice peeling away layers until you identify your deepest emotion in any given situation. Next, develop courage to tell those closest to you how you really feel. Don't say, "Nothing," when someone asks what's wrong. If you react in anger because you're afraid, give yourself the gift of vulnerability. Tell them, "The more scared I am, the more mad I sound." If you feel frustrated, speak up and say why in a respectful manner.

- Facing your feelings produces much discomfort. Anytime you succeed, celebrate. Reward yourself by doing something you enjoy. You've earned it after hard emotional work.

Practical Help

- Money issues are signs of deeper difficulties. Safehorizon.org, a victim assistance organization touching the lives of more than 250,000 affected by crime and abuse each year, is a great resource for helping you unearth a buried past, while offering fresh solutions for symptomatic problems.
- Do everything possible to ensure a good night's rest. Go to bed at the same time every night. Darken your bedroom completely. Cover windows, digital alarm clocks, or anything else emitting light, as this interferes with your body's production of melatonin, the natural hormone providing deeper and more restful sleep. Under the supervision of a physician, if all else fails, you may consider taking an occasional melatonin supplement to help you cycle through a complete night's refreshment.

- Sit your spouse down and have a very honest discussion about your true financial condition. Create a budget together. Samples are available at anitabrooks.com. Visit Crown Financial Ministries, www.crown.org, ChristianFinancial Ministries, www.christianfinancialministries. org, or another accredited financial institution for more tutelage in how to release yourself from the bondage of consumer debt.

Spiritual Comfort
- From cover to cover, the Bible tells us to "take courage" (see Matthew 14:27). This is active, not passive, a verb we are meant to pursue. Jesus speaks to us, saying, "Don't be afraid. Take courage. I am with you!"
- Practice patience with yourself. The temptation to mentally browbeat yourself over emotional trauma is powerful, but resolve to love yourself so you are equipped to love others through action. Take comfort—God in His grace knows how weak we are. He remembers we are made of dust (see Psalm 103:14).
- God surely understands what we're fighting to repress, for He knows the secrets of every heart (see Psalm 44:21).

GUIDED PRAYER

Dear Jesus,

I praise You for understanding my struggle against the past and for teaching me how to take courage in my present. Thank You for making the desire of my heart to please You over any woman or man, and for Your guiding hand taking me to the right resources for relief from my current situation.

CHAPTER 5

Spread Too Thin

M aybe you're one of them.

"We have to make changes. I'm sorry, but we don't need you anymore." These words have rung in the ears of many men and women who find themselves unexpectedly laid off from work.

"We have no choice—it's a matter of solvency." Shocked employees learn their livelihoods will soon ship overseas.

"We did our best," the owner says as the lock latches for the last time on a closing business.

Have you experienced one of these scenarios? Any or all of these statements cling to our psyche, leaving an imprint of subliminal and insidious PTSD symptoms. The blanket of job security rips off our shoulders. Questions pummel our brains. Will we find work again? Will we lose our home? Will we lose our cars? Will we have money to feed our children? In a health crisis, will our families receive life-saving care?

Even when we've survived a series of job cuts, another round of downsizing, or a reengineering overhaul, we still live under the threat of the ever-sharpening global financial pencil. Will the ax fall on our necks next?

And then there's survivor guilt. A shadowy beast

nibbling at our insides while we strain to protect ourselves against future threats, new and dangerous realities.

All of these undercurrents play against our productivity while company leaders, feeling their own pressures with fewer people to provide brawn and brains, push us to work longer hours.

We try to shield ourselves with mental mantras such as "It is what it is." Or "I just have to deal with it." While at our core, in a place deeper than we let ourselves think about, our emotions subconsciously drive us to act out of our dread. We strive to get everything done, when the reality is that there aren't enough bodies with enough on-the-job experience to pull it off.

Without realizing we've done it, along with the fat, we've cut the meat of stability and the heart of trust in our globally reduced workforce. After all, technology is only as good as the minds propelling it. The essence of our financial skeletal system is damaged when humans are disregarded as unnecessary parts. And wounded people are left with a bitter taste languishing in their mouths. Sometimes with dangerous consequences.

Recently, after speaking at a business conference about how work affects home and home affects work, a woman from the audience approached. I'll call her Molly. She asked to talk with me, so we found a quiet corner in the hotel coffee shop.

She fidgeted with her cup as she started talking. "It's been over a year, but I can't seem to adjust. I can't get over the changes."

I leaned in to show my concern. "Tell me what happened."

"I was at my desk working through another lunch when I heard Wanda before I saw her. She's the human resources manager.

"She said, 'Can I see you in my office?'

"I nearly choked on my egg salad sandwich. But she didn't make eye contact with me. Instead, she nodded at Bret. He used to sit one desk over. Poor guy; I could tell he was stunned.

"Wanda sounded firm, but I noticed a shake to her voice when she said, 'Right now, please.'

"Bret popped up like a jack-in-the-box."

A server interrupted Molly's story to see if we wanted anything else.

"No, thank you," we said simultaneously and then smiled at each other.

"Please continue," I encouraged.

"I was scared. I can't remember if this was the third or fourth round of layoffs, but I'd been through it before. So had Bret. I shuffled some papers, trying to look busy, intentionally avoiding eye contact with Wanda. Hoping it would protect me.

"In my peripheral vision, I could see Bret fumble with a file folder. He asked, 'Do I need to bring anything?'

" 'No. This won't take long,' Wanda said.

"Rumors had flown for weeks, but now I was watching it unfold. And I felt like I was going to lose my lunch right there on the desk."

Seeing the tremble as Molly raised her latte to her lips, I reached out and rubbed her free hand. Research had told me a brief exchange of appropriate physical touch helps some traumatized persons feel relief when reliving their memories. Healing energy is exchanged in nonsexual, skin-to-skin contact. Knowing Molly's issue wasn't sexual or physical abuse, or the result of serious combat-related PTSD, I took the chance. Her soft smile at my touch said I'd made the right decision.

She continued. "Twenty minutes later, Bret shuffled to his desk, and Wanda was walking behind him with an empty brown box. His face was blank, and his eyes were dark. His lips were thinly drawn, chalky white."

Molly swallowed hard and looked down. "I can still taste the bile that crawled from my stomach into my mouth. After Bret left, they let two more go. All I could do was pretend to work. Anything I did that day was inferior at best, and that scared me. I just knew Wanda would come find me next. I thought the day would never end, but finally it did. I snatched my purse and rushed out the door as quick as I could, before Wanda could give me a pink slip. By the time I got home, I was too wiped out to think about dinner. Thankfully it was Wes's turn to cook. He's my husband."

"How long have you been married?" I wanted to give Molly a mental break from the weight of her story.

"Eight years. He's a great guy. Supportive. Caring. Except he really made me mad that night."

"How's that?" I knew she was ready to share more details.

"After we ate, we parked on the couch to watch the evening news." Molly took a big breath. "The anchor sounded so glib. How do they do that? Wes says you get hardened—as an EMT he's seen a lot. Anyway, the newscaster said, 'In Minneapolis, a gunman walked into Accent Signage Systems just hours after he was fired.' Isn't it weird I can remember the exact name of that company?"

"Not really." I brushed a crumb off the table. "In some instances of trauma, particulars imprint on our minds. It's also common for us to go blank on other details, no matter how hard we try to recall them."

Molly exhaled loudly. "Anyway, the newscaster wasn't done. He reported matter-of-factly, 'About 4:25, the former employee drove back to Accent Signage, parked his car, and walked to the loading dock area, spraying bullets in that location. Witnesses say his face was expressionless.' "

Molly rubbed her arms as if she were cold. "I turned to Wes and said, 'Another one? It seems like every day someone goes into a school or office with guns blazing. We're not safe anywhere. Those poor people—and their families.'

"But Wes didn't respond like I thought he should.

" 'Don't let it get to you.' He sounded as if he didn't care.

"I told him, 'But people died.'

"He tried to console me. 'That shooting took place in another state, hundreds of miles away. It doesn't have anything to do with us.'

"I guess I was supposed to feel comforted, but instead it made me mad. I pulled back, turned on him, and said, 'How can you sound so cold? They're human beings. Besides, you didn't see the expression on Bret's face today. His eyes were hollow when Wanda walked him to his desk. What if it happens where I work next? Are you going to act like it's no big deal if I get shot?' I knew that would get to him.

" 'I'm not cold. But I can't afford to worry over every little thing.'

" 'People dying is not a little thing,' I told him.

"He paused, like he was trying to figure out how to respond; then he said, 'I'm sure Bret won't do anything, but just in case, let's go over the list.' He always thinks he has to fix me."

Molly paused, so I nodded to let her know I was following the story.

"He has this catalog of things I'm supposed to remember if I'm ever in danger from a shooter. It drives me crazy. One extreme or the other. He either blows things off, as if I shouldn't worry about anything, or harps at me like I'm a child.

"I guess I rolled my eyes, because he reprimanded me and said, 'This is serious.'

"I told him, 'I know. I'm the one who started the conversation. Remember?'

"He acted like I hadn't said anything and kept talking. 'Never sit or stand with your back to the door. If you hear bullets, don't forget runners have the highest survival rate in a shooting. Don't freeze, don't try to grab your belongings, just get out as soon as there's a safe opportunity. Try to run in a zigzag crouched pattern. Don't stop to call 911, do it while you're on the run if possible. If you can't run, then barricade yourself in a room. Turn off any lights. Stay away from the door once you've locked and blocked it. And focus on staying calm while you wait for help to come.'

"I told him, 'I'll probably forget half of that.'

" 'You'll remember when you need it if you review things in advance.' He held out his arms for me. 'Now stop worrying; you'll only make yourself sick.'

"I snuggled in, but I told him, 'I already feel sick.'

"Of course he's got an answer for everything. He told me, 'You can't spend your whole life afraid. Ninety percent of what we fear never happens. Besides, you're more at risk of losing your job than of someone like Bret snapping.'

" 'That's comforting. What are we going to do if I get fired?'

" 'We'll deal with it then.' For Wes the discussion was over. He pulled away and turned back to the TV.

"But I couldn't let it go. No matter what he said, in the privacy of my own soul, I knew I was in for a sleepless night. The next day I was exhausted and as jittery as a squirrel. It felt like my adrenal glands were working overtime."

"No doubt they were," I affirmed Molly.

"It took a few weeks for the worst of my nerves to simmer down, but even after all these months, I can't seem to shake a cloud of dread. I worry someone our company fired will turn into a maniac or I'll lose my job. Neither one of those things has happened—yet. But what if?

"And if that's not enough, there's another problem I am dealing with."

"Oh?"

"We don't have enough people to do the work required. They expect a third of us to accomplish what an entire team of people did before. I live in a constant state of fatigue. I can't move as fast as they want—to do the job accurately. But if I don't do my work well, my head may end up on the chopping block. I feel like I'm on a hamster wheel and I can't get off. And there's more."

I leaned forward, allowing my body language and a quick "Mm-hmm" to spur Molly further.

"The other day, Wanda told me our company is making plans to reengineer again. In a different way. And it could make things even worse.

"In preparation for the Affordable Care Act, they plan to hire several new people, but hours will be cut across the board to reduce the number of full-time employees. She says she's not supposed to tell anyone the real reason, but they're doing it to avoid paying health care benefits so we can stay in business. The sad thing is, I work in finance, so I understand the reasons behind their plan. Our company is in the small to medium range, and our budget is already tight. The money going out is growing while our income is shrinking."

Molly took a deep breath. "But from an individual

standpoint, what about my family? We're living week to week as it is. I can't afford to have my hours cut."

As Molly finished sharing her concerns, I commiserated. Lately I'd heard multiple stories of a similar nature.

Molly was feeling the aftershocks in a downsized company where the remaining staff is spread too thin, laced with frustration and anxiety over changing policies. To add further post-traumatic tension, she felt that her family and friends didn't take her concerns seriously.

In today's society, we've convinced ourselves that multitasking works, although it proves less effective than concentrating on one project and seeing it to conclusion. Having fewer full-time, experienced workers means weaker work teams. But how do businesses sustain themselves without pushing to get more done with less?

As a business coach, I believe PTSD is an invisible killer of productivity in the workplace. Add rising costs, an increase in governmental regulations, and other profit-choking expenses, and then you understand why pressurized leaders are as stressed as those they are supposed to guide.

I hear from employers and employees, and they both make valid points. Those in leadership are concerned about keeping the bottom line black, finding and retaining a workforce with integrity, and keeping up with a global economy in warp-speed change, while trying to lead their own meaningful personal lives.

Yet the people who work for these leaders bear their own burdens. Much like Molly described in her story, employees wonder if they'll have a job at the end of the day—a valid concern, but one individuals can affect.

In my book *First Hired, Last Fired: How to Become Irreplaceable in Any Job Market*, I share principles to help immunize employees against the global pandemic of job loss. Using stories, practical tips, and encouragements along with relevant passages from the Bible, I show readers what employers really want. Whether they realize it or not, the answers leaders seek exist in the Bible's ancient text—where I've found more than eight hundred scriptures related to prosperous work.

The Bible is a balm when our spirits are wounded or worried. And after assuring Molly that her responses to downsizing and an increase of workplace violence were natural, I directed her to some of my favorite scriptures, applicable to our twenty-first-century problems.

I told her, "Deuteronomy 28:12 says, 'The LORD will send rain at the proper time from his rich treasury in the heavens and will bless all the work you do. You will lend to many nations, but you will never need to borrow from them' " (NLT). I felt my eyebrow arch, a signature move when I get really serious. "Of course you have to read the entire context because God created the natural laws of cause and effect, decision and outcome, choice and consequence. This means you can't expect a blessing if you disregard His rules for successful living."

Molly looked puzzled. "What do you mean read the entire context?"

Sometimes I don't recognize a Christianese statement when it slips out of my mouth. So I clarified. "Sorry. It simply means to read the passages before and after the one you're focused on. In this case, I recommend reading all of chapters 26 through 30 in Deuteronomy."

"Oh. Okay." Molly wrote the book name and chapter numbers on a napkin. But she still had a puzzled look on her face.

"How about if I share a simpler concept?"

Molly's eyes lit up.

"The New Living Translation of Ecclesiastes 5:5 says, 'It is better to say nothing than to make a promise and not keep it.' "

"I try to keep my promises," Molly defended.

"As do most people." A man I recognized from the conference walked by and smiled. I smiled back.

"But here's what strikes me about Ecclesiastes 5:5. How many times do we tell someone we'll do something but fail to follow through? You see, whether we use the word *promise* or not, when we've created an expectation, others have a reasonable belief we will keep our word. This scripture holds us accountable. It also empowers us to offer a gracious no when we're pressured to say yes to something we shouldn't."

"Makes sense." Molly added the scripture to her napkin.

"Psalm 127:1–2 stops me from fretting. It doesn't do any good. God's in control, and believing Him takes the pressure off."

Molly turned her napkin over after scratching the passage address on it.

"Proverbs 14:23 promises hard work will lead to profit, while mere talk leads to poverty. Isaiah 46:10 reminds us that God knows the end before anything starts. Again, it's a trust thing."

Molly wasn't looking at me anymore, but her head kept nodding as if to agree while she scribbled. "Got any more?"

I thought for a minute. "I almost forgot one of my favorites. Joel 2:21–27. I love the part where it says God will give back what the locusts have eaten. Think about that word picture—He can resurrect and recreate anything circumstances have destroyed. I've learned to ask God to redeem my lost time, energy, relationships, and resources. He created everything from nothing, so it makes sense that He can restore."

Molly jotted the name and numbers, then said, "I've never heard anything like that."

"As a culture, we're not reading the Bible as much today, so we're missing out on a lot of encouragement and empowerment. It's a shame."

She laid down her pen. "I'm not a Bible reader. In all honesty, I'm not sure I believe it's anything special. Just another book. Not that we can't learn from reading, but a book inspired by God? No offense, but I'm not convinced. After all, a bunch of people wrote it. It's more like compilation stories, right?" Molly looked at me with expectancy.

I chuckled. "I used to harbor those same kinds of

doubts. As a matter of fact, I was pretty vocal about my skepticism. But one day I realized something critical."

"Which was?"

"I was spouting off on a subject I wasn't knowledgeable about. I'd never read the Bible for myself. So I made a commitment."

"To?"

"To read the entire Bible. Cover to cover. It took me a year, but I followed one of those reading plans, like the YouVersion app for your smartphone or tablet. And when I was done, my entire perspective changed. I realized no one is that intelligent. No group of people has the wisdom or the ability to see into the future the way the Bible does. After reading it for myself, I know why some people say it's alive. I have yet to find a problem it can't help me with."

"But I've heard people say it's hard to understand."

"I struggled a fair amount in the beginning, but I committed to not giving up. I kept reading, and over time I started grasping more."

"You sure seem to understand it now."

"Believe me, there's a whole lot I don't know yet. But I keep learning. It's another biblical success secret you can add to your list. Along with one more scripture."

Molly poised her pen.

"James 2:26. It relates to everything else we've talked about. You see, God tells us faith without works is a dead faith. It's meaningless. We must partner with God. He doesn't feed us intravenously; He expects us to work and gather the blessings He wants to give us. When we choose to believe Him, we act like it."

She started to tap the ink pen against her temple as if embedding our conversation in her mind.

I continued. "I'm not telling you what to do, I'm simply sharing what's worked for me. But what can it hurt to give the Bible a try when you get scared? Will you be any worse off if it doesn't make a difference? But what if it would help, and you missed out?"

I could feel my passion for the subject getting the better of me, so I apologized. "Sorry. I didn't mean to come on so strong, but when you know something works, you just want everyone else to experience a great thing."

Molly smiled. "I'm really glad you took the time to talk to me. I don't know how things will turn out, but I have hope for the first time in months. Thank you."

We visited a little while longer and then went our separate ways. Last I heard, Molly said things had improved. She's sleeping and eating better, and she told me, "I feel more peaceful than I have in a very long time."

She reported her company was still grappling with their downsizing efforts, but they had refilled some positions where they previously let employees go. They'd even rehired some, as leadership recognized the value of experienced people they'd lost, knowing it would be more expensive to start from scratch.

As I write this, Molly's company hasn't felt the full impact of the Affordable Care Act. She isn't sure how it might change things, but she has newfound confidence that God will carry her and Wes through. She also said she's praying regularly for the leaders in the business she works for.

We live in uncertain times, and sadly, post-traumatic stress has become so commonplace many of us don't recognize it for what it is. Instead, we heap false guilt on ourselves, feeling worse because we feel bad.

Some like Wes, who work directly with trauma victims every day, can suffer from an even lesser known condition: compassion fatigue, also known as secondary traumatic stress (STS).

Secondary traumatic stress is characterized in a person by a gradual lessening of compassion over time—unless it is directly related to them. Common among physicians, psychologists, and first responders, it was first diagnosed among the nursing community in the 1950s. Sufferers exhibit a sense of hopelessness, an inability to experience pleasure, sleeplessness, night-mares, and an increasingly negative attitude. It can produce detrimental effects, both professionally and personally, as a lack of focus along with feelings of self-doubt rise. But you don't have to work in the medical field to experience it.

A growing number of journalism analysts say the media is causing widespread compassion fatigue among everyday members of our modern society. In a world saturated by news, reported with dramatic flair and available in real time on all manner of digital devices, we are bombarded by verbal and pictorial images of tragedy and human afflictions. This may explain why cynicism, self-centeredness, and a resistance to helping those who are suffering are on the upswing.

Though we live in an era of unprecedented communication streams, lack of emotional awareness and poor training add risk to jobs and lifestyles associated with periods of high stress or a single traumatic incident. A culture of silence is the unspoken rule for most who experience either mild or major trauma. Those who've suffered don't want to talk about it or others don't want to hear.

Chronic worry and compassion fatigue, both milder symptoms of PTSD, should be taken seriously. Over time they wreak havoc on home and work relationships, undermining our peace and productivity. Our hope lies in taking intentional steps to acknowledge and deal with our emotions through healthy practices so we don't waste a lifetime wondering why other people find happiness but we cannot.

Much of what we fear never happens. But if our worst fears do become reality, we can get through, many times becoming stronger in the process. We can follow the example of those who survived what many of us can't imagine.

Let your adversities shape you into a person of compassion who uses your past to help others in the present. Don't believe you are not needed—you are. Decide to make a fresh start with fresh faith today, looking for purpose in your pain instead of allowing it to paralyze you from living. Unearthing one reason to smile or reading a powerful scripture can get you through a single moment when a whole day is too much to think about. But to find them, you first have to look.

One thing we don't have to look for are security concerns—a drive to protect basic needs so powerful we often don't realize what or why we're fighting. In the following pages, we'll discuss what happens when we lose the very roof over our heads—homelessness can happen to anyone.

INSIDER INSIGHTS

Emotional Healing

- Listen to "You Are" by Colton Dixon, especially if you aren't sure what to talk to God about or how to talk to Him.
- Plan something fun, whether you feel like it not. We all need regular doses of something to anticipate. When we've lost the ability to enjoy ourselves, to play, sometimes a change in habit can help us find our way back to the feelings we desperately desire. If nothing sounds pleasurable, return to a childlike activity like finger painting, swinging, flipping a Frisbee, or playing tag with your mate or a friend.
- Go on a mission trip or get involved with a charitable agency. Experiencing another's need in person is different from watching it from a distance. When you put your faith to action by helping drill for fresh water, feeding the hungry, or rebuilding after a natural disaster,

it can transform the way you feel. Hope is restored in us when we restore it for others.

Practical Help

- Take intentional mental breaks from whatever increases your stress. Close your eyes and imagine a relaxing scene. The smell in the air, the colors of the sky, the sounds in the air, the tastes on your tongue, the touch on your skin. It costs nothing to take a mental break in your favorite happy place and come back refreshed.
- For centuries, color has been used for healing. According to many experts on the psychology of color, shades of green relieve stress and enhance a sense of tranquility. Blues soothe and reduce pain. Orange increases energy levels. Yellow stimulates the nerves and purifies our thinking, while red arouses our bodies and minds with vitality, increasing circulation.
- Spend ten minutes making a list of your current problems, breaking them into lists under headings of things you can control and things you cannot control. Take progressive action on at least one thing you can control, and choose to release those things you have no way of affecting.

Spiritual Comfort

- Take a sabbath rest from all digital devices, including television, at least one day a week.

Is there anything that can't wait twenty-four hours? Jesus tells us the Sabbath is made to help people, more than just a rule to keep (see Mark 2:27 NCV).

- If God owns the cattle on a thousand hills, know He owns the gas in a thousand tanks, the jobs in a thousand companies, and the groceries on a thousand shelves (see Psalm 50:10).

- In our twenty-first-century culture, we aren't tapping into the power of holy healing through fasting and prayer, where chains are loosed, cords are broken, and the oppressed are set free (see Isaiah 58:6). What can it hurt to give God's way a try?

GUIDED PRAYER

Dear God,

I don't always understand why things happen. Thank You for knowing what I need and providing it. I praise You for peering deep into my fears and leading me to healing strategies, for restoring what I've lost.

CHAPTER 6

Homeless in Seattle

From birth we fight our way through life for one intrinsic thing. We take offensive action when necessary—we defend to the death if that's what it takes to protect it. We don't stop until we believe it is safe. We equally want to know we can provide it for the people we care for.

What is this desperate need driving us from the core of our souls, even when we don't realize what we're doing or why?

Security. Knowing we are loved, accepted, and free. Confident in our creative endeavors. Secure in meeting our basic needs for oxygen, water, food, and shelter.

And yet, we're one relationship, one war, one physical or mental illness, one breath, one drought, one famine, or one foreclosure away from losing what we've fought so hard to protect.

Any one of us could choose an item from the list of things that make us feel secure and say, "My worst fear is losing this."

To combat those fears, we try to preoccupy our minds with a myriad of things. Busyness. Denial. Overindulgence. Avoidance. Disdain.

For instance, take Wendy, a woman I recently met at an inspirational women's conference. After I spoke, she asked for a few minutes to tell me her story. We found a less frequented hallway and sat down. She smiled sheepishly while smoothing a strand of black bangs falling across one of her deep blue eyes. She looked at her lap more than at me as she started talking.

"I grind my teeth at night. I can tell because my mouth feels sore every morning, and I feel the release when I stretch my jaws like this." Wendy demonstrated by rounding her red lips in a large oval. After a few seconds, she continued, "Did you know most of us hold as much tension in our jaws as we do in our necks and shoulders?"

"No, I didn't."

"My doctor told me that."

"How fascinating." I found myself moving my jawline, and sure enough, realized I hadn't noticed the rigid weight residing there.

"Yeah. But by doing mouth stretches throughout the day, it helps release my pent-up tension. My doctor taught me that too."

"Interesting."

"It gets really bad when I grind my teeth, though. I don't realize I'm doing it, but it keeps me from getting a good night's rest. I spend a lot of my waking hours feeling fatigued. My doctor says I do it because of trauma."

"How were you traumatized?"

She pulled a few strands of invisible lint from her skirt before talking. "I used to feel proud of where we lived. We had a house in the country club district."

I noted the slight droop to Wendy's shoulders when she paused.

"In all honesty, I looked down on people who were from a certain part of town. My husband, Tom, had made a lot of money while he was still in college. He's super smart. Brilliant actually. So by the time I met him, he was already established. That was over twenty years ago."

"What does he do?" I asked.

"IT. When he started in the field, it wasn't saturated like it is today. Now it seems like everybody and their uncle works in technology." Wendy picked at more lint that wasn't there.

"Information technology certainly has expanded."

She continued. "In the months prior to Tom losing his business, we changed our lifestyle dramatically, thinking we could salvage what we'd worked so hard for. I'm a teacher, so we still had my income. Not enough, but sufficient to give us hope in the beginning.

"At first we didn't want to sell the house. Part of our identity was tied to our possessions. Now don't get me wrong—we didn't live in a mansion, but we had a nice life. Before everything fell apart.

"It took almost a year for us to exhaust our savings, max our credit cards, and extend our line of credit. When things reached the point of having to decide between eating our next meal or putting gas in the car so Tom could look for work, we knew we were in big trouble. For a while, we still thought we might keep the house. Soon enough, that illusion faded too.

"I called a Realtor recommended by a friend. The agent came to look at the house, and I was encouraged by her promising statements. 'Very nice,' she oohed over the sun porch we'd added.

"She made notes on her clipboard while she asked questions and offered compliments. 'You say the flooring is new?'

" 'We installed it a little over a year ago.'

" 'Great.' She jotted something indistinguishable down. 'Any exterior improvements in the past five years? Roof? Windows? Gutters? Doors?'

"I thought of the improvements we'd made, one by one, year after year, savings after savings. Through my memory, I relived our laughter as Tom and I added fresh pink paint in Bethany's room. How accomplished we felt when the new landscaping was done. I remembered our son, Jason's, face the first time he slid across our new wood flooring.

"I squelched an impulse to shove the woman out the door, twist the lock, and bar her from reentering. But then my stomach growled, and I remembered why she was there. So instead of giving into my impulse, I answered her question. 'All of the windows are less than five years old. We took advantage of the federal tax credits for energy-conserving home improvements.'

" 'Good. Good. Major interior additions?'

" 'The wood floors were installed last year. We replaced the furnace about four years ago.'

" 'Great. Is there anything else I should add to the sales sheet?'

" 'I can't think of any.'

"The real estate agent made her way to the door. 'Give me a ring if anything else comes to mind. But even with the rocky market, I think your price point is strong, and I'll be surprised if we don't have a buyer within a few weeks. Or sooner.'

"After she exited, I leaned against the door, taking in the scent of After the Rain, my favorite air freshener. I allowed myself to believe the Realtor's optimism. But she was wrong.

"One month turned into three, so our agent lowered the price. Tom still hadn't found a new job, but at least we were eating. In addition to my day job as a teacher, I had picked up a part-time position as a cashier at our local Chick-fil-A. The first time one of my students came into my line, I thought I'd pass out from humiliation. But I took his order instead.

"That night I cried in Tom's arms. But we weren't necessarily in it together.

"The fights were bad. They ebbed and flowed, dependent on whether the most recent news was hopeful or terrifying. We argued over everything from our messy house (neither of us had the energy or desire to clean), to helping the kids with homework, to whether Tom was really looking for work or just lying around. I suspected he spent more time watching television than job hunting.

"Every day it felt like we were losing more control. And as my ability to guide my own life slipped away, so did my confidence.

"Practical things I had taken for granted like utilities, gas in my car, food in my stomach, water to drink, a hot shower, clothes for my children—everything was in question, and my emotions didn't like it. When my daily comforts and necessities started to disappear, it made me feel like I would disappear. It didn't take long for things to affect me physically.

"Previously a solid seven- to eight-hour sleeper, now I was fortunate if I got six hours. I could barely eat, which was a blessing with our tight food budget. When I did grab something, it wasn't good. It's expensive to eat healthier, so I started living on candy bars and sodas for energy. I felt lousy.

"When the attacks started, I knew I was in real trouble. The first time it happened, I thought I was dying. Tom took me to the emergency room. I wondered, was this a heart attack? Was I having a stroke?

"After they ran several tests, the attending physician came to see me. She adjusted her stethoscope and said, 'Everything came back normal. Is there anything unusual happening in your life?'

"It was rude, and I didn't mean to snort, but I did when I told her, 'That's like asking if your coat is white.'

" 'I'm willing to listen.' She smiled warmly, and it melted the iciness I felt. A little.

"I straightened my spine and stretched my neck higher. 'My husband just found work after losing our business, but at half the pay. I'm working two jobs. I don't see our kids other than yelling at them to get ready for school or to brush their teeth before bed. We used credit cards to buy groceries and pay the mortgage. Now they're maxed out. We can't afford to do anything fun anymore. We're all miserable. And there's something else. Something I haven't told anyone.' "

Wendy bit her bottom lip before continuing. "I told her, 'I fantasize about running away from my family. All of them. Husband. Kids. Extended family. I dream about cashing my paychecks, but instead of buying food or paying bills, I just hop in my car and drive. I go until I can't go anymore, and I end up in some city where no one would ever think to look for me. Someplace I've never been or talked about. And then I lose myself in the crowd and start all over. Fresh slate. Clean start. Blissfully alone, no one else to care for.'

"I asked the doctor, 'Isn't that the most self-absorbed thing you've ever heard?'

"I was surprised to feel her reach out and touch my arm. I looked up to see glistening in her dark brown eyes when she said, 'You don't sound selfish to me. You sound like a woman in survival mode.'

"I told her how exhausted I was from trying to keep up. I whined, 'Our son needs new shoes, but I don't know how I'm supposed to buy them. We've eaten more peanut butter and jelly in the past few months than any of us have consumed in our entire lives before. We're dangerously close to losing our house. And honestly, I'm not sure how I'm going to pay you.'

"She said, 'Don't concern yourself with my bill. There's help for people in your position.'

"A lump formed inside my chest. 'But that's just it.

I don't want that kind of help. We should be able to pay our own way. We always have.' I felt perspiration form above my lip and an intense burn firing up in my belly.

"The doctor stood. 'Tell me what you're feeling right now.'

"My airway was closing off quickly, so I sputtered, 'This. . .is why. . .I came. Sometimes. . .can't catch. . .my breath. Feel. . .like. . .going. . .to die.'

" 'Try to stay calm.' The doctor came alongside me, lifted both of my arms above my head, and began to rub my back gently in swirling soft circles. 'Keep your arms up. Slow your breathing. Ease air into your nostrils slowly, counting to ten as you inhale.'

"I tried to focus so I could obey the doctor's instructions. The triple-fast beats of my heart didn't help.

"She kept rubbing my back, and I must admit it helped a lot. 'That's it. Good. Now exhale. Just as slowly through your mouth. One. . .two. . .three. . .four. . .five. Gently. Gently. Six. . .seven. . .eight. . .nine. . .ten.'

"I could feel some of the surface tension releasing.

" 'Now, let's do it again.'

"I began another inhale through my nose.

" 'Slow down. Don't breathe too fast.'

"The soothing effect of her voice seemed to guide my emotions as much as the slow breathing. Within minutes the relief was palpable. I could feel a knot of anxiety still balled up inside my chest, but at least I wasn't suffocating.

"I sounded like I'd just run a marathon, but at least

I could speak in full sentences. I asked her, 'What's wrong with me? Is it my heart?'

" 'We'll run a few more tests before I give you a diagnosis, but I suspect you're experiencing symptoms of an anxiety disorder induced by the trauma of your changing financial condition.'

" 'Anxiety disorder?'

" 'In laymen's terms, panic attacks. They're notable for a sudden rush of physical symptoms. Shortness of breath. Muscle spasms. Nausea. Burning sensations. Dizziness or light-headedness. Choking impressions. Shaking. Sweating. Fatigue. Weakness. Hot flashes or sudden chills. Tingling in your extremities. A fear you are going crazy or that you might die. Terror of crowds or terror at being alone. Heart palpitations. A sense of being smothered.

" 'You might feel several of these things at once or have a pattern of consistently encountering only one. But no matter how few symptoms you might experience, they are always coupled with uncontrollable anxiety and sometimes an impending sense of doom.'

" 'Why are they happening now?'

" 'Think about all the traumatizing things rolling through your mind. Your husband's job loss. Separation from your children now that you're working multiple jobs. Your perception of yourself as a less than ideal mother, even though you are exhausted physically, mentally, and emotionally. Escalating debt. Worries about whether you'll have food to eat. Concerns about losing your home. And who knows what else. An onslaught of panic attacks makes perfect sense to me.'

" 'Is there a cure?'

" 'Let's make sure this next round of tests comes back negative, then I may want to prescribe an anti-anxiety medicine.'

" 'Do I have to take a pill?'

" 'You don't have to. Many people find relief using more natural methods, but some serious cases do require medical assistance. I'll give you a pamphlet on anxiety, and you can also do your own research. I just urge you to follow the advice of credible experts. Investigate options thoroughly to ensure any treatments you consider offer tried and tested solutions.'

"I thanked the doctor and felt relieved when I left her office. A few days later, she called with the new test results, confirming I didn't have a major malady.

"But the good news did nothing to reduce the intensity of my attacks, blindsiding me at school, sometimes forcing me to excuse myself in front of my students. One caused me to park a shopping cart in the center of an aisle, groceries inside, while I fled for fresh air.

"I did find a few remedies online, mostly breathing and muscle-relaxing techniques. I started walking since exercise was listed on every site I visited. And these things did help. Some. But not enough. How could they? With our worst fears crashing on top of us?

"The Realtor was wrong. Our house never sold. The notice came in the mail on a Tuesday. It stated a Notice of Default was filed, and we were in a reinstatement period, running until five days prior to a foreclosure auction. We were informed if our mortgage wasn't current within ninety days, we would lose our home.

"After that, we received a Notice of Sale. It was physically posted on the house, filed with the County Recorder of Deeds, and published in local newspapers for three weeks. The notice said a foreclosure sale date had been established, and our home would be sold to the highest bidder. Any deficiency between our loan balance—including interest, late charges, and other fees—and any winning bid outside of our bank would fall on us to pay.

"During those ninety days, besides pushing the Realtor to sell the house at a reduced price, we desperately applied for refinancing. To no avail.

"For weeks we sat across from bankers we'd known for years, as well as with men and women we'd never met before, to hear variations of the same things. 'I'm sorry. Tom hasn't been on his job long enough. Your debt-to-income ratio is too high. Even if your balances weren't at limit, your open credit potential is too risky compared to your salaries. Your recent history has lowered your credit score substantially. I wish there was something we could do.'

"We loaded the last boxes on a Saturday evening. Some of our larger belongings were stacked inside my parents' garage, the rest stuffed into the shed in their backyard. The remnants of clothes, shoes, jewelry, and toys left after yard sales went with us. Two adults and two young teens shoved into my in-laws' basement.

And we thought we got on each other's nerves before!

"Even with all of our scrimping, we still had to sell our newer vehicles. Now we're both driving cars over ten years old. I hated the humiliation, especially when I pulled into a parking lot next to one of my old neighbors. I felt like an outsider where I lived, but I couldn't go home.

"The hardest part was watching my children suffer. They couldn't have friends over. Getting ready for school in the morning was hard, since there's only one bathroom in my in-laws' whole house. That meant Bethany set her alarm for five thirty to take her shower, fix her hair, and put on makeup. A tenth-grade girl works hard to fit in, and my heart ached for her. I know she was embarrassed. Jason required less prep time, but he still had to get up forty-five minutes earlier.

"I used to shower in the mornings, but I became a night bather. A mama's gotta do what a mama's gotta do. Tom worked the evening shift at the hospital, so at least he could avoid the bathroom rush, although it was a lousy schedule for our marriage. We hardly saw each other.

"I finally broke about a month after we moved out of the house. I went back to see the doctor and accepted her prescription. But it made me so drowsy I could only take it right before bed; otherwise I'd fall asleep at the wheel or at work. I hated the foggy tired feeling that followed me all day long. So I started looking for alternatives. And I found my answer in an unexpected place.

"When things started falling apart, I started going to church. By myself at first—Tom and the kids thought I'd lost my mind, but I was actually trying to save it. I'd never attended church, but I called a friend who did, and I went with her one week." She chuckled as if at an insider's joke. "Desperate people do desperate things."

"I'd never experienced anything like it, and it was invigorating. The minister seemed to read my mind, but I knew he couldn't possibly know my problems. No one there did at first; even my friend had no idea why I asked to join her.

"The first time I went, my friend introduced me to another friend of hers, and the three of us developed a tight bond right away. It was as if we'd known each other our whole lives.

"One day a few weeks later, I was waiting in the pharmacy line when I got this group text from one of them. It said, Look up Philippians 4:6. The answer for what worries us.

"Curious, I tapped my Bible app. I'd loaded it at the minister's suggestion but hadn't bothered to use it before. I'm new to all this church stuff, so it took me a few seconds to navigate the Search button, but I figured it out and typed in the Bible book, chapter, and verse.

"At first I was a little puzzled at what I read. 'Don't worry about anything; instead, pray about everything. Tell God what you need, and thank him for all he has done' [NLT].

"I liked the part about not worrying and telling

God what we need, but thanking Him for what He had done didn't sound right to me. How was I supposed to thank Him for losing everything? But I kept reading it. Slowly. Over and over. Oddly, just doing that seemed to calm my nerves so that by the time I got my prescription, I no longer felt like I needed it.

"The next time I was with my friends, I told them a little bit about our situation. Not all of it, but enough. They were both so sweet. Then I told them how the text with Philippians 4:6 had calmed me. One of my friends started wiggling with excitement.

"She said, 'Let me teach you how to meditate on it.'

"It sounded a little weird, so I just said, 'Meditate?' I have to tell you I wondered if this was some kind of New Age thing.

"But my friend laughed, and said, 'Meditation just means to concentrate deeply. The Bible mentions meditating a lot.'

" 'Okay,' I told her, but I still wasn't sure.

" 'Here's how you do it. Slowly read the passage multiple times, but focus on one word each time you do. For instance, while reading the first part of Philippians 4:6, concentrate on the word *don't*. Like this, "*Don't* worry about anything." Now you try it.'

"So I copied her. '*Don't* worry about anything.'

"'Good,' she said. 'Now, concentrate on the second word. "Don't *worry* about anything."'

"'Don't *worry* about anything.'"

"'Great. Now the third one. "Don't worry *about* anything."'

"I could see why she was excited. 'Don't worry *about* anything', I repeated.

"'Don't worry about *anything*,' she finished.

"'Don't worry about *anything*.' I get it. The whole structure of the sentence changes when you do that. It's like God is telling you something different each time."

"'Exactly.'

"After that, I was hooked. I started reading the Bible more. There were a lot of things I didn't understand at first, but my friends helped me. Then one of them told me about James 1:5, where it says, 'If any of you lacks wisdom, you should ask God, who gives generously to all without finding fault, and it will be given to you.' So I asked for wisdom. I even meditated on that scripture, and it worked. I'm learning more all the time.

"But the greatest thing is, I don't have anxiety attacks anymore. When I recognize one trying to start, I hurry to look up a Bible passage; then I meditate on it. And it works. Better than any medicine and no side effects.

"Things are also turning around for us financially—slowly. We're easing our way out of debt. We just moved into a nice rental house. It's small and not in the country club part of town, but I don't care anymore.

"Tom and I are happier. He's started coming to church with me sometimes, and when he does, the kids come too. I'm a better mom, more balanced in my thinking. I've realized it's good for our children to learn about overcoming adversity. I used to cushion the blows for them, but it hindered their ability to handle the real world. I think they're all wondering what happened to the grumpy worrywart that used to live with them."

With that, Wendy wrapped up her story. As she finished, I thought of all the other Wendys and Toms who were struggling to get over the loss of security in their homes.

In January 2014, *CNN Money* reported that residential prices were rebounding and foreclosures were on the decline.[6] But for the thousands who've already lost their homes, this good news is nothing but a sad reminder—a trigger taking them back to the agony of losing their earthly possessions. Leaving them with an emotional punch in their guts.

When any of us face financial troubles, we step onto a tightrope. And we can teeter in two directions. On one side, we swallow our pride and overcome our shame. While we work, sacrifice, and strive, we also accept help. One humbled choice at a time, we move toward a better ending to our story.

But some of us fall on the opposite side. We feel sorry for ourselves and blame governments, ministries, and other people when our needs aren't met. Justifying all manner of avoidance, rather than intentionally choosing to meet our obligations—one penny at a time if necessary.

God's plan includes abundance in our lives. Not necessarily wealth in monetary measures, but riches in love, joy, peace, forbearance, kindness, goodness, faithfulness, gentleness, and self-control. This is the fruit of His Spirit according to Galatians 5:22–23.

Meditating on His promises, knowing your past need not define your future, taking steps today that will build, eventually leading you out of the valley of despair. This is the path to true security—where safety isn't dependent on where we live, but on Who we know. This is where lasting freedom resides.

But sometimes who we know is the problem. When power, possessions, and properties are involved, devotion can turn into hate. In the next chapter, we'll discuss the age-old problem of family feuds.

Insider Insights

Emotional Healing

- Our healing song for this chapter is Switchfoot's "This Is Home." No matter where you rest your head, a brand-new mind-set can lead you home.

- Anger is grounded in fear. When the fights start over money problems, and especially as they escalate, ask yourself this question: "What is it I fear most?"

- Join a support group for those in similar circumstances. Keeping your feelings bottled up can magnify negative thoughts and fuel dangerous explosions. Check with hospitals, doctors, therapists, financial agencies, or online forums to find gathering spots for people who truly understand what you're going through.

Practical Help

- Rework your budget. Instincts will drive you to avoid facing your finances, but the best and fastest way to crawl toward recovery is one decisive action step at a time.
- If job loss is part of the problem, update your résumé. Study tips for acing an interview. You can find "Top Job Interview Questions and How to Answer Them" on my website, anitabrooks.com.
- One corner and one hour at a time, declutter your life. Depression can drive us to let things fall apart. But a cluttered environment leads to a cluttered mind. Break the cycle by cleaning up.

Spiritual Comfort

- "Fear of the LORD leads to life, bringing security and protection from harm" (Proverbs 19:23 NLT). God's promises strengthen us when we are weak.
- Many have suffered homelessness, experienced bitter emotions, and hit bottom, but knowing we are not alone helps us grip hope so we can continue on (see Lamentations 3:19–21).
- Our Father's house has plenty of room (see John 14:2). Jesus is preparing a special place where one day we will worry no more. He will wipe away our tears and allay all fears by providing a permanent home, a mansion— security no one can strip away.

GUIDED PRAYER

Dear Father,

You are my provider—not an employer, not a government, not any organization or person. But I realize I must work with You to meet my needs. I will meditate on Your Word and follow Your direction, trusting You to secure my hope and a good future.

CHAPTER 7

Family Feuds

I t's a story as old as God's creation of time and humankind. Greed. Jealousy. Sibling rivalry.

The great thief of inheritance. The great murderer of relationships. The great destroyer of peace.

A rash of news reports reveal a deepening rift in family bonds—especially when perceived power or valuables of any kind are involved. In some cases, blood is not thicker than money. Whether real or imagined.

These days a life insurance policy may be all that's required for someone to consider murder. Or for family members to accuse when there's no evidence to support foul play. Deceitful emotions can tear grieving loved ones apart.

A core of competition flies from our souls when we believe there's something personal at stake. Fear of losing what we believe we're entitled to can decimate all semblance of residual family love.

Family ties can also stimulate unrecognized PTSD symptoms, creating triggers. Making us susceptible to doubt, paranoia, and an increase of melodramatic encounters with those whom we've shared meals, births, holidays, health, and sickness. Trusted confidants transform into bitter enemies.

Lines are drawn. Sides are taken. Wars are waged.

Assumptions, allegations, accusations—these are the ties that blind us.

Les Kotzer, a Canadian attorney and author of *The Family Fight: Planning to Avoid It*, recounts the story of a client whose mother believed she had no assets of any lasting value. Always broke, the mother made no inheritance stipulations after her death. For her children, this was a costly relationship mistake.

After her passing, a parcel of letters from former US presidents was found in the woman's house. They turned out to be worth a substantial sum, and a lasting feud began between her children.[7]

This case may sound extreme. But whether possessions, caregiving, or another issue escalates resentments, surprising reactions can manifest through grief. Most families have faced or feared the conflict that can occur when Dad or Mom passes away. All it takes is one person to prioritize stuff over relationships—or so it seems—and the battle begins.

You may or may not believe it could happen to you, but the following story is not exceptional.

Her granddaughter, Katie, stood near her head on the right. Her daughter, Melina, on the left. Thelma's breathing came less often. And when it did come, it came in softer blows.

Melina smoothed strands back to the top of her mother's forehead, allowing her fingers to linger on clammy skin. "It's okay, Mama. You can let go."

A muffled moan answered, or was it imagined?

A tear slipped down Katie's flushed cheek. She

leaned down and brushed a kiss on her grandmother's face.

A sudden commotion caused them to look away from the dying matriarch. One thud followed another, sounding like a heavy purse and clunky shoes dropping to the floor. The crinkle of shopping bags fell next. Norma filled the doorway—in typical dramatic flair. She narrowed an intent gaze at her sister and daughter. "How long have you been here?" Norma directed the question to her older sibling.

Melina steeled herself, hoping her mother was oblivious to another round of unnecessary squabbling. "Not long."

"What? You don't think I can take care of Mom?"

"I never said that."

"It's what you think."

"Can we not do this now? I think we should focus on Mom, don't you?"

Norma sneered. "This isn't all about you. I'm her daughter too." Norma made her way to the bed and nudged Katie out, not bothering to acknowledge her daughter in any other way. She made a show of dropping a sloppy kiss on her mother's forehead.

"I'm fully aware." Melina sighed.

"Mom wants me in charge of seeing her wishes are met."

Melina recognized her sister's manipulation but suppressed the inclination to call her out. It would do nothing but heighten the tension, something Melina wanted to protect her mother and niece from. "I don't want to argue with you. We need to make the most of our time with Mom."

Katie walked to the foot of the bed in silence.

"Where do you think you're going?" Norma directed heat at her daughter.

"Just giving you room next to Grandma."

"I know you're taking her side." She nodded toward Melina. "You always do. Ungrateful, that's what you are."

Melina opened her mouth then closed it. Instead of speaking, she left—not just the room, but the house. She would spend the rest of her life regretting it. Her mother passed in the middle of the night.

For the most part, the funeral was a foggy blur. Melina shook hands and smiled courteously at those who wanted to share a warm or funny snippet of their time with her mother. Katie stood near her aunt, while Norma, Kleenex in hand, clutched every mourner who passed by, standing close to the casket. Her outbursts at the graveside were even more theatrical.

Melina was grateful for the chance to leave Norma's cloying act behind. She left the cemetery depleted of all energy and went home to grieve in peace. Or so she thought.

For a couple of weeks, Melina's closest friends stayed near while Norma kept her distance. But after each person eased away, slipping back into their own daily routines, Melina was rocked once again, robbed of solitude and her chance to mourn privately—because a new type of grief was coming.

When she saw Norma's name on her cell phone,

Melina's instinct was to ignore the call. She was tired enough to speak unconstrained, knowing it was volatile. But she hit the Answer button anyway. "Hello."

"We need to see Mom's lawyer. So she can read us the will."

A rock sunk in Melina's belly. "Can't it wait?"

Norma shrieked in response, "No!" Then with a calmer tone, "Let's just get it over with."

"Fine. You make the appointment and let me know when."

"I will." Melina noticed the cheery lilt as the phone died. Typical.

A few days later, seated in high leather-backed chairs across from a blond intellect, Melina, Katie, and Norma faced the attorney. With a warm yet professional tone, the woman began to read. But Melina wasn't fully prepared for what the document said.

By the end of the reading, Melina's right knee shook uncontrollably. Once again, and in a final blow, their mother showed favoritism to Norma. Why a lifetime of conditioning didn't prepare her for the inevitable, she didn't know. But Melina was still stunned.

The attorney cleared her throat periodically as she read, "I leave my house and all its furnishings to Norma, in hopes she will take the opportunity to start over. Upon my death, all of her debts to me are considered paid in full. She is also to receive my certificate of deposit held by Peoples Bank in the original amount of ten thousand dollars, along with any accrued interest." The lawyer lifted a piece of paper sitting next to the will and said, "After compounded interest earnings, the current balance is twelve thousand one hundred nine dollars and forty-five cents."

Norma gave her sister a sideways sneer.

Melina felt heat creep along the tops of her ears.

"To Katie, I bequeath my car and savings account." The attorney picked a document off the desk near her left hand. "As of the last statement cycle, that balance was four thousand six hundred twenty-two dollars and nineteen cents."

Katie didn't look as pleased as Norma had. But Melina knew mother and daughter didn't share similar motives. Her niece would not trade her grandmother's life for a car and some cash.

The attorney wiggled in her leather chair, causing it to squeak. "And to Melina, my faithful child, I leave you my antique trunk, filled with personal treasures I've accumulated throughout my lifetime. I hope you cherish them as much as I have."

Melina waited. Surely there was more.

The attorney looked up and smiled. "Any questions?"

"Yeah," Norma said.

"Figures," Melina muttered.

After scowling at her older sister, Norma challenged the woman seated at the desk. "What's in Mom's trunk?"

"You mean *my* trunk." Melina relished a moment of power over her irresponsible and self-centered sister. Then she felt guilty for acting childish and letting her sister push her buttons so easily.

Ignoring Melina's intrusion, Norma pushed the

lawyer again. "So what are the mysterious treasures of a lifetime Mom left in that trunk?"

"I have no idea," the woman answered gently. "Your mother didn't leave an inventory of its contents." The attorney held out her hand toward Melina, a small brass key nestled on her palm.

Snatching it quickly, in case Norma tried to take the only thing their mother had left her, Melina viewed the key curiously. What *was* in that trunk?

Melina's thoughts were interrupted by the attorney who covered a few final loose ends, handed each family member a certified copy of the will, then excused them. As they left, no one said a word, but the two sisters practically raced to the exit door.

Melina got the jump out of the parking lot and called her husband on the way to her mother's house, to help heft the trunk into her car. And for protection, in case Norma decided to act out. Which, of course, she did.

Using the door key still on her ring, Melina unlocked her mom's house one final time. She stopped just over the threshold, feeling something inside her chest squeeze her heart like it was a wet rag. A hand clamped her right shoulder, making her jump in response.

The sound of her husband's laughter struck a nerve.

She wheeled to face him. "It's not funny. I was thinking about Mom."

His face instantly drooped. "I'm sorry, honey." He reached out and gave her a hug.

"Let's just get Mom's trunk and get out of here. Maybe we can escape before Norma shows up."

"Sure." Her husband followed her up to the attic.

They had made it halfway across the driveway when the police arrived. Two officers opened their doors and approached. "You need to stop where you are," the graying policeman said.

Melina and her husband cautiously rested the old trunk on the white graveled driveway. "We just came to get my property, and we're leaving."

The younger officer held up his hand in a stopping motion. "A report was called in from"—he pulled his phone out and looked at the screen—"a Norma Potter, stating you are trespassing and anything you've taken from the house is stolen property."

"This is ridiculous." Melina threw her hands in the air.

"Calm down, ma'am," the first policeman said.

"You might want to tell her that." Melina pointed as Norma's tires dug into the driveway while she jerked her car to a stop.

She started yelling before she'd gotten out of her vehicle. "See, I told you she was here to steal from me!"

"You're a liar." Melina knew she sounded like a ten-year-old.

"Am I?" Norma waved a piece of paper as she walked toward the police. "This is a certified copy of my mother's will, giving me full ownership of this house and its contents." She turned to face Melina. "You do not have permission to enter without my authorization."

The way Norma sounded, Melina expected her sister to stick out her tongue.

Taking a breath to settle her nerves, and hoping she could communicate at a more mature level, Melina made another attempt to speak with the officer in charge. "If you read toward the end, you'll see my mother bequeathed me this antique trunk. It's the only thing she left me, and my sister is trying to take it as well."

"What's your name?" The policeman flipped through the will.

"Melina."

"Do you have your driver's license on you for identification?"

"I do." Melina slipped her purse off her shoulder and dug her wallet from the bottom while Norma shrieked.

"Hey, I'm the one who called you. This is *my* house. She didn't have the right to go inside *my* house without my permission. You should arrest both of them for breaking and entering."

The officer kept his voice calm. "How did you get inside, ma'am?"

"I used my key." Melina held out her ring, pulling the house key prominently apart from the others.

He turned to Norma. "There was no breaking and entering, ma'am."

"That key belongs to me now. I don't want her to have one to my house."

"Take your stupid key." Melina twisted and turned

the ring, freeing the silver object. She tossed it in the general direction where Norma stood, and it tinkled as it landed on the ground at her feet.

Norma stooped and picked it up, leering at her older sibling as she did.

The police officer interrupted. "According to this document, you are entitled to the trunk. But you should have gotten your sister's permission to enter the house first."

"She wouldn't have given it," Melina countered. "The trunk would have mysteriously vanished, along with everything inside."

"Whatever." Norma bristled.

"I suggest you and your husband finish loading, make peace with your sister, then leave."

Norma scoffed. "Peace? With her? We're grown women, and she still thinks she can tell me what to do. But I'm over it—and her. Mom's not here to play referee anymore."

Melina shrugged her shoulders, tired of her sister's games, then turned and looked at her husband. "Are you ready?"

"Okay."

Together they lifted the rust-encrusted box off the ground and carried it to their car. When they pulled away, Norma's rants echoed behind them.

But the trouble wasn't over between the sisters. Norma made numerous threats to file a lawsuit against Melina, forcing her to disclose the contents of the trunk.

In reality, there wasn't anything of monetary value

inside. Melina half hoped she'd find a personal note from her mom, revealing why her actions seemed to favor Norma, but really meant something else. She ached for a mother's expression of deep and everlasting love for her oldest girl. But amid stacks of family history, letters between her mom and dad, baby books, vintage photos, and albums filled with snapshots of her and her sister, Melina didn't find that note. She took her time going through what was there.

When she got to their family albums, Melina spent a whole day flipping through the pages. Two towheaded tots three years apart and seemingly connected at the hip smiled from the first crinkly sheets. A familiar but distant affection stirred in Melina's chest.

The next stage of their lives showed Melina and Norma between ages five and ten. Birthday parties, splashing under a water hose, playing with their cousins at a family reunion, climbing the oak tree in their backyard. Their natural personalities were beginning to show through their clothes. Melina dressed in carefully coordinated earth tones, while Norma mismatched bright polka dots, pastel stripes, and dark plaids.

A photo of both girls folding laundry made Melina stop flipping. She recalled the way her mother clucked over the tiniest of flaws on her part. Norma, a master manipulator, would work to get out of work until their mom would say in exasperation, "Just go on; I'll do it myself." But she never let Melina off the hook.

She knew their mother had meant well. She was forever trying to fill whatever void Norma couldn't fill for herself. But coddling had only permitted self-centered behaviors to grow, often at Melina's expense. At least that's how she saw the situation.

Melina slammed the album shut. She resolved to put the past behind her. Her life would not stop for someone who only thought of herself.

In that moment, she decided not to give her sister the satisfaction of knowing what was inside the trunk. Let her wonder. She didn't know her decision would haunt her. Some choices once acted on can never be altered or taken back.

Norma died a few months later when a deer leaped onto the interstate where she was driving, crashing through her windshield. Authorities said it happened more often than people realized.

Melina took it hard.

Thinking back on the altercations between her and her sister, where she'd seen justification at the time, Melina now saw childish behavior—on her own part as well as Norma's. The recurring dream started the night of her sister's death.

Melina was chasing Norma up the scratchy bark of a tree. The girls were about nine and six. Norma scooted onto a limb, but Melina wasn't worried because her sister had a yellow rope tied around her waist, a precaution in case she fell. They were both laughing, and six-year-old Norma was taunting in her dainty little voice, "Can't get me. Can't get me."

The teasing made Melina crawl faster. She reached the limb and grabbed for Norma. When she did, her younger sibling lost her balance, screaming as she plummeted. The rope broke her fall, but it also broke something else. In Melina's hellish feature, the rope instantly transformed into a noose, choking off Norma's laughter.

Then Melina would wake up. Drenched. Heart palpitating. Reliving the final moments in that gnarled oak tree again.

Anxiety was eating Melina inside out—the effects evident on her body. Her eyes were sunken, her face drawn, tension lines deepening. One day in particular, she sounded nearly suicidal when a good friend dropped by.

"My emotions are all over the place. I'm confused. Mad. Depressed. And I feel guilty, even though I did the best I knew how at the time."

"Isn't that normal?"

Melina snickered. "What does normal look like?"

"Good point," her friend agreed.

"Maybe I'm getting what I deserve."

"What do you think you deserve?"

She rubbed both hands up and down her face. "Punishment, I guess. For the bad blood between Norma and me. For petty competition over Mom's affection? It all seems so silly now that Norma's body lies cold in the ground. How can I forgive myself for my selfishness? I wish I could turn it all off."

"You aren't thinking of hurting yourself, are you?"

Melina's eyes watered. "Sometimes, but I don't think I'd really act on it."

Her friend prodded, "How long have you felt like

this? You do know you are needed, don't you?"

Melina snorted. "All I do is make a mess of things. Nobody needs me."

Her friend grabbed her hands and squeezed. "Don't let your emotions lie to you. You are helpful, kind, giving, and compassionate."

A sigh fell from Melina's lips. "Maybe I used to be that person."

Her friend squeezed her hands again and said, "I don't claim to understand everything you feel, but I can tell you what I know. You are important. Hold off one more day. One more hour. One more minute. Give God a chance to pull you through."

"I believe in God. I'm just not sure what He thinks about me."

"He loves you. You've made mistakes—we all have—but you have done nothing He is not willing and waiting to forgive you for. The question is, will you forgive yourself?"

Melina sobbed.

Her friend hugged her and whispered through her hair, "I can't fix you. Ultimately your wounds are between you and God, but I can support you. You matter to me. Please know how many people would hurt if we lost you. Don't make us live without you in our lives."

They sat for a very long time together in silence. When she was ready, Melina shared a few more intimate details about her struggles while her friend simply listened.

During the following weeks, Melina's friend texted

her an encouraging quote, prayer, or scripture a couple of times a day to let her know she was thinking of her. Slowly, Melina improved, one moment at a time, until one day her friend received a call asking if they could meet. A new energy reflected in Melina's voice.

"A few nights ago, I prayed before going to sleep, 'God, teach me how to forgive Norma and myself.' "

"Oh?"

"The next morning I woke up feeling more hopeful than I had in a long time. I hopped out of bed and sat down with a Bible, a notebook, and a pen. I started scribbling, trying to keep up with the thoughts coming from my head. This is what I wrote:

"People love me conditionally, but God loves me unselfishly. People let me down, but Jesus lifts me up. People offer me advice, but the Holy Spirit offers true wisdom. I can cry on someone's shoulder, but only God can permanently dry my tears.

"Then I Googled 'Christian forums for toxic relationships.' After twenty minutes, I found an online group I liked and joined. Next I searched, 'What does the Bible say about toxic relationships?' I read articles and started comparing them against passages they referenced. I found a lot of helpful information.

"Then I took my notebook and wrote this heading: 'What I Need to Do to Heal.' I was stunned at the bullet points on the page when I finished."

- Seek God daily instead of ignoring Him and trying to do things on your own.

- Study scriptures about relationships. Ask these questions about each one: What's beyond the surface of what you're reading? Who was this originally written to? Where is this taking place? When did things change? Why is this relationship significant? How does this apply to you and your relationships?

- Revisit your childhood and ask yourself if there's any unresolved grief. Were you wounded, betrayed, or damaged without going through all of the mourning stages necessary for healthy healing? If so, allow yourself to grieve now.

- Take inventory of your relationship with Norma and Mom. What things from your early years caused problems in your adult relationship with each of them? Are you harboring demons of fear, false guilt, shame, or hate?

- Understand Norma's manipulation originated from insecurity. You acted appropriately when refusing to give in to her unrealistic demands.

- Recognize Mom did the best with what she knew. It is possible she loved you equal to Norma as she said, just uniquely based on who you are, different from your sister.

- Remember that repentance is more than saying I'm sorry; it's showing it through a consistent change in your actions and offering symbols of your remorse. You cannot take responsibility for Norma's choices, but you can love her in spite of her faults.

- Accept Amos 3:3, "Can two walk together, unless they are agreed?" (NKJV). Because you and Norma didn't share similar values, core beliefs, purpose, and goals, you couldn't agree with each other while she was alive.

Melina sighed. "Can you believe I wrote all of that in a matter of minutes?"

"Sounds like you had a lot bottled up."

"That was just the start. I flipped to a new page in my notebook and wrote: 'Steps I Can Take to Forgive Myself Now.' Then these spilled from my pen."

- Stop wallowing in false guilt. You tried to resolve your differences with Norma. You would have run to her side if she genuinely needed something.
- Confess without condemnation your specific demons of hate, fear, shame, and false guilt to God. Analyze them bathed in the light of His love, realizing He sees your wounds and how you've reacted from them, versus how you see yourself. He was with you when the hurts began, and He is with you as you heal.
- Ask others what positive traits they see in you; then write their affirmations on Post-its. Place them on your bathroom mirror, your refrigerator, in your car, and any other place you frequent.
- Refuse to be ashamed of you. Give yourself

permission to love yourself wholly, accepting your flaws as part of your human condition while equally accepting goodness as part of who you are.

- Don't assume you know how God feels. If He says you or others are forgivable and you say differently, you are telling Him you know more than He does.

- Surround yourself with healthy friendships, godly counsel, and joyful encounters. Plan outings and adventures where your spirit can soar.

- Allow yourself to smile, or even better—to belly laugh. Spend a whole day with someone who makes you happy.

Melina smiled widely. "When I looked at everything I'd written, I saw it as a healing outline, something I can refer to or add to as needed. I'm still grieving, but I'm not a slave to it anymore."

Part of Melina's journey included a fight against herself. Sometimes she felt okay, but much of the time she hated herself for feeling bad. Especially when blindsided by a PTSD trigger.

Certain smells, a photograph, a visit to her childhood home, the taste of cookies like her grandma's favorite recipe, a melody—any one of these could throw her into a dark or enraged mood. But once Melina faced her past conflicts and practiced forgiveness, an ongoing process she cycled through many times, she made it through her valley.

Melina learned that if you want to increase your happiness in the present, you must resolve your yesterdays and prepare for your future. She recently said, "The final lines in the pages of your life are written by what you choose today." Wise words.

Because God allows us to participate in the writing of our own stories, including the endings, we must realize our relationships with others play major parts in each scene. Cast the roles carefully. Don't let unhealthy distractions prevent you from being all you are meant to be. But equally, don't play the narcissist, making life solely revolve around you. Find the healthy balance prescribed throughout the Bible; apply what you learn; and at your final breath, know that you did your best as God carries you into lasting freedom.

Betrayal of any kind is a painful thing, especially in the relationship between husband and wife. If ever there was something impossible to get over, it is true of the affairs in marriage. In our next chapter, we'll watch as one couple claws for hope when a wife's worst nightmare shoves her into a shadowy valley. Can she make it through? Only turning the page will tell.

INSIDER INSIGHTS

Emotional Healing

- "Need You Now" by Plumb is a great song when we need help but don't know how to move forward on our own.
- Instead of focusing on what you don't have, can't do, or how others are lifted up when you

feel let down, concentrate your thoughts on your positive qualities. What is pure, good, noble, or lovely in you? Resolve to live true to your best self.

- Follow Lucille Zimmerman's advice in her fantastic book *Renewed: Finding Your Inner Happy in an Overwhelmed World*. On page 30, she encourages readers to watch a movie, such as *What's Eating Gilbert Grape*, where there are many family members interacting in stress-filled situations. Early into the film, find one character you identify with and journal your feelings. It's a powerful experience.

Practical Help

- Call a family meeting. Find out who places the most sentimental value on what items—revelations can surprise you. Have the patriarch and/or matriarch make an inventory of their possessions, listing who should get what on their passing. Remember, these possessions are theirs to give. Determine not to place importance on things over people.

- Look at those who bring out the worst in you with a new perspective. What might they fear? Why might they strive to put others down to make themselves feel better? What void are they trying to fill with their poisonous actions? Resolve to pity them versus play into their games.

- Timeline the highs and lows of your life. Through adult logic, ask yourself if the way you remember events is based on verifiable facts or simply your emotions. Do you have any responsibility in broken relationships? Where appropriate, have you shown your remorse in your words, but more so by your deeds? Have you detoxed from unhealthy relationships and distanced yourself in healthy measures—loving the sinner, even as you hate the sins?

Spiritual Comfort

- Think about all the people who are impacted by your conflicts. Those indirectly involved, but also those who get pulled into emotional tugs-of-war. For the sake of your family and friends, let "peace be within you" (Psalm 122:8).
- Choose harmony as much as it depends on you (see Romans 12:18). Sometimes we forget we can influence—but can't force—change on others. If someone disregards your attempts at a truce, offer a gentle "I'm afraid we'll have to agree to disagree," then walk away from further entanglements.
- Let God's mercy, peace, and love multiply for you (see Jude 1:2). Ask and listen for His guidance. If you want to have a conversation with God to hear what He wants to say to you, then go where He is sure to speak—and listen.

GUIDED PRAYER

Dear Father,

You know I want to do the right thing, even though I don't want to be walked on or treated like a doormat. So, in faith, I thank You for pulling the roots of bitterness from my heart and planting flowers of forgiveness in their place. I praise You for helping me live in peace, including with those who use me or otherwise treat me badly, and showing me when I need to love them from a distance.

CHAPTER 8

The Affairs of Marriage

T he scene is played out in countless movies and
television shows. A hint of a smile. An electricity-
brandished brush against an arm. A promise in a
flirtatious, fluttering eye. A quick glance over a coffee
cup. A shoulder to sniffle on about perceived marital
woes. Until finally they trap themselves with the first
whisper in an ear, followed by an illicit kiss.

Until you've been on the receiving end of adultery,
these scenes may cause mild interest or your heart
to palpitate with growing anticipation. You might
even empathize with the unmarried lovers. But once
you crawl unwillingly into the skin of the deceived,
something as simple as a movie can instantly transform
you from a gentle soul into a raging lunatic.

The intensity and speed of the transformation is
shocking. Like a werewolf exposed to moonlight, when
betrayal is illuminated, your hackles raise, your hair
stiffens, snarling fangs replace your sweet smile, and
the claws come out. The sight isn't pretty—for you most
of all.

Affairs come in many forms—long-term sexual
encounters, short trysts, overnight dalliances, emotional
connections, phone sex, pornographic fantasies, online
meet-ups, sexting—but it's all adultery. Cheating takes

what we believed about our most intimate relationship and rips it to shreds.

According to an article titled "The New Workplace Romance," published by Focus on the Family, the highest percentage of extramarital affairs occur between colleagues who work directly or indirectly with each other.[8] Regular exposure in the workplace often affords the complicit parties more time together. In our twenty-first-century culture, most men and women spend the majority of their waking hours working outside the home. Not all cheat, but the percentage of those who do is high.

In some cases, the offending spouse shows immediate remorse and fights to win their wounded wife or husband back. Sometimes it takes a while before the adulterer realizes what's really at stake and is ready to display humility along with a repentant heart.

But there's a sad reality. Many of these gut-wrenching stories end in total marital destruction. Stubborn refusal to think of anyone but oneself causes the unfaithful to chase illusions of love through lust, leaving a trail of smashed dreams and shattered lives. Often they become the most miserable of all.

Whether our spouse stays or leaves—regardless of financial status, educational background, nationality, personality, or gender—marital infidelity rocks us to our core and can drive us kicking and screaming toward post-traumatic stress disorder. A place where we have an absolutely normal reaction to an abnormal amount of stress, even though we may feel like we're losing our minds.

The murder of marital trust guarantees serious consequences. Without profound healing, we can suffer for a lifetime. But with intentionality, we can step into a place of personal restoration.

With or without our partners in our lives, we can become whole again. We can relearn to laugh. We can seek and find joy. We can even discover how to love as if we'd never been hurt. We can get through a traumatizing event no one ever gets over—but it does require patience with yourself, outside support, and the affection of the One who is never unfaithful.

In case you question it, the Faithful One does exist, as Denise found out. Her story proves we can once again step into light after walking the dark valley of marital infidelity. It takes more than two to make a marriage work—it takes three.

She feared it more than death. Adultery.

Denise had a reason for her foreboding: her dad had had an affair when she was a teenager, taking a piece of her heart when he walked out the door to move in with the other woman.

For more than seventeen years, Denise fought a silent war within herself, hoping if she was a great wife—not perfect—but good, she could prevent infidelity in her own marriage.

She tried to fulfill Sam's desires, even if they sometimes clashed with hers. She pretended to like sports on television when she would have preferred to watch a good murder mystery. She wore clothes he picked out instead of ones she felt comfortable in. At his request, she put makeup on every day, though she felt the sting of not being good enough as she was. When Sam disciplined the children harshly, she soothed their tears with tender yet supportive words. "Shh, your daddy loves you. He just wants you to do better."

Lately Sam was on edge, as if he were looking for a fight. At least four times a week they replayed the same scene. Denise begged him to tell her what she was doing wrong, but he'd rake his fingers through his hair and bark, "Nothing. Nothing's wrong!"

"But you act like you're mad at me. Can't we talk about it?"

Averting his brown eyes from hers, he'd say, "There's nothing to talk about. Now quit nagging me."

And with those final words, the guilt would rise like hot oil in her throat. Denise would shut down—until fear triggered another pleading outburst.

Between arguments, Denise tried a fresh approach. Shaping her brunette hair into the style he liked, applying his favorite purple eye shadow to enhance her gray eyes, painting lipstick over her pasted smile, she'd ask, "Do you want to go for a walk or to the movies?"

"No."

"Let's go away for the weekend. Just you and me."

"I don't feel like going anywhere. Do something with one of your friends."

"I want to spend time with you."

"There you go, nagging me again."

Sam's accusations confused Denise. She wasn't trying to nag. This wasn't about her. It was about the two of them. About working for a happy marriage. About showing their children stability and joy through positive family experiences. But lately she couldn't seem to say anything right. Sam turned everything into a battle. He seemed depressed and miserable and determined to make the rest of his family join him.

Many nights Denise cried into her pillow so Sam wouldn't hear. His lack of concern made her feel lonely and scared. They were living the definition of insanity, doing the same things over and over, expecting a different result.

Try as she might, Denise couldn't understand what was going on with her husband. All of her attempts to make things better only made them worse. And then, on a sticky summer night in late June, Denise got her answer. And it would change her life forever.

They were up later than usual. He was getting ready to take a shower, and Denise had just grabbed a fluffy white towel from the laundry basket, snapping it to fold. The phone rang, and she glanced at her watch before mumbling, "Who could be calling this late?"

She picked up the receiver. The firm voice on the other end belonged to a man she didn't recognize. "Is Sam there?"

"May I ask who's calling?"

"James Walters."

"Just a minute." Denise shrugged and thought to herself, *It's probably one of Sam's employees calling off work tomorrow.* She put her hand over the phone's mouthpiece, walked down the hallway, and knocked on the bathroom door. "You've got a call."

Through the door, Denise could hear Sam growl, "Who is it?"

Feeling attacked, defensiveness edged Denise's words. "He said it was James Walters."

The bathroom door creaked open, but just a few inches. Sam reached through the tiny opening so only his hand and wrist were visible.

Denise slapped the telephone on his palm then walked back to the living room where she proceeded to fold her whites. She was smoothing the second one when Sam called her name.

Now she groused as she tromped back down the hallway. "You'd think his legs were broken. Can't put the telephone back for himself."

She arrived at the door. Once again, only Sam's hand slipped through the thin crevice of opening, receiver waving in the air.

Thinking he meant for her to hang it back up, she started to snatch the phone, but Denise noticed the signal light was still on. Confused, she paused and stared at the red dot, trying to process the oddness of the situation.

Sam's muffled voice rattled her. "He wants to talk to you."

"Who does?"

"James Walters."

"But I don't know him."

"Talk to him."

"What did he say?"

"He said I'm a dead &¢*!*&¢!. Now take the phone."

Shocked into timidity, Denise carefully pulled the receiver from Sam's hand to her ear and stumbled back to the living room as she spoke. "Hello?"

"Mrs. Martin?"

"Yes."

"Ma'am, I hate to be the one to tell you this, but your husband is having an affair with my wife. It's been going on for over a year."

The floor started spinning beneath Denise's feet. "How do you know?"

"I've got recordings."

Prickly sensations attacked Denise's entire body. Then a surge of hope filled her belly. "You must have him mixed up with someone else."

Movement in the corner of Denise's eye caused her to turn toward the kitchen. Sam stood in the dark. Shirtless; barefoot in a pair of jeans. Head hung toward his exposed chest. His eyes wide, round, and doe-like.

The clock seemed to stop ticking. All of her senses shifted to high frequency. Denise noticed how the scent of fabric softener blended with ripening bananas from her kitchen table. A rich metallic flavor coated her tongue. Her body felt light, as if she'd stepped into a different dimension. She knew.

The man on the phone was talking in a whisper of deep compassion. ". . .no mistake. It's him. You seem like a real nice lady, and I'm sorry."

Through stabs of white-hot pain beginning to pummel her chest, Denise felt a faraway appreciation for the stranger's expression of kindness. His protectiveness, where her husband had failed to protect, wasn't lost on Denise. In a daze, she said, "Thank you for calling."

"Take care of yourself, ma'am."

"I will."

A quick click, and the call ended. But the war was getting ready to begin.

Denise put the phone on its cradle and looked at Sam, a sliver of desperation still clinging in her mind as she dared the question. "Is it true?" Denise held her breath, wanting the impossibility. That he would answer, "No."

But Sam nodded slowly, and in a hoarse voice, he said, "Yes."

Then he moved into action. Fast strides, holding his arms open in an offer of comfort.

Denise stiffened. "Stop. Don't come near me, and don't you dare touch me." Emblazoned thoughts lit her brain like machine-gun fire. *Now he wants to show me compassion? Where were his hugs when I asked for them? All of these years, trying to please him, trying to make him happy, going along with everything he wanted, and this is the thanks I get? He knew. Of all people, he knew.*

Sam stopped halfway between where he'd been and where Denise stood.

She gritted her teeth and ground out her words. "Of all the ways you could hurt me, this is the one thing I begged you not to do. You knew what I went through when Daddy left. You promised you wouldn't do this to me. To our children. To us."

Sam's shoulders drooped. "I know."

"Who is it? Tell me."

"I don't want to hurt you more."

"It's too late for that."

Sam swayed as if Denise's syllables had been swords, stabbing his body. Then he slumped. "Linda Walters. You met her at the Christmas party last year. She and her husband sat diagonally across from us. In the red dress."

Stunned, Denise let the questions forming in her mind take flight through her mouth. "The trashy-looking bimbo you work with? The one I asked you about because I saw the way she looked at you? The one you told me to quit being stupid over because you'd never cheat on me, especially with someone like her? And you remember the dress she was wearing?"

"Let's not talk about this. I don't want to make things worse."

Denise bristled. "How dare you. You think talking about it will make things worse? You've already committed the worst. You and that slut killed our marriage. How did this start anyway?"

Sam kept his voice even and calm. "Don't blame someone you don't know."

"So now you're going to defend her?"

"I'm not defending her, but I don't want to see you like this."

"Well, too bad. You created the situation." Denise stationed her hands against her hips. "And you didn't answer my question. How did this start?"

"I don't think hearing the details is going to help."

"You obviously don't care about what helps me. So save your fake concern, and tell me how you started sleeping with the whore at work."

Sam sighed loudly. "Fine. We just started talking. Normal stuff. Work projects. Family. Kids."

"You discussed our children with her? They are none of her business. You won't even talk to me about our children! God knows I've tried to get you to communicate about them."

"I know, Denise. I don't need to hear it."

"Apparently you do. You broke a sacred trust by discussing our children with her. And who knows what you've said about me! About us. Why wouldn't you come to me? I begged you to talk to me."

"I guess because she didn't get worked up."

"That's because she has nothing invested in our family. She doesn't love our kids like we do. She can tell you what you want to hear because she doesn't care. I do. You're supposed to."

"I didn't see that. She seemed like a nice person. That's all."

Sam's words stung. A new thought almost knocked Denise off her feet. Though she shed no tears, because her ducts felt dry, a knot formed in the depth of her throat. With narrowed gray eyes, she targeted Sam's brown irises. "Do you love her?"

His eyes shifted away from hers. "I don't know. I mean, no."

Cold horror washed through Denise's veins.

"Which is it? No, or you don't know?"

"No. I don't think I love her. I love you."

"Think? You don't think?" Feeling the walls close in, Denise surveyed the room, not processing what she was doing, not realizing she was looking for an escape.

Sam restarted his approach unnoticed. He got to her before Denise realized he was coming closer. His embrace was powerful as he whimpered in her ear, "Babe, I'm sorry. Please forgive me."

Forgetting the kids were asleep at the end of the hall, Denise flung his arms off her and screeched, "I said, don't touch me! You gave up that right when you touched *her*! If you have a problem with it, I suggest you look in the mirror."

Sam's tears weren't dry like Denise's. They glimmered and made his brown eyes more prominent. "I deserve that."

"Yes, you do. I've got to get out of here. I can't look at you right now." Denise spotted her purse and started fumbling through it as she headed toward the door. She felt the jagged edges of cool metal and gripped her car keys. She glanced back at Sam. Feeling torn, a part of her never wanted to see him again. Another part still loved him. She couldn't switch it off. She ached for him to swoop her into his arms and try to stop her.

But with chin quivering, Sam said nothing. He stood there, accepting her repulsion as penance for his sins.

Denise turned, walked outside, made her way to the car, and got in. She started the ignition. And as she pulled the gear into Reverse, she took one more look toward her home. Then she froze.

In the doorway, Sam stood silhouetted by their living room light. But he wasn't alone. Three smaller bodies stood in front of his, stair-stepped in height. Thirteen, eleven, and eight—huddled against their father. It was the oldest whose hands cupped his face. Denise could tell Lee was sobbing. And she wanted to bolt from the car so she could tell her little boy everything would be all right. But she couldn't make that promise. Instead, guilt heaped on raw wounds. She backed out of the driveway and drove into the night, toward no particular destination.

Denise drove for hours. Old memories wrestled against new emotions. She remembered the day her daddy walked out. She wasn't much older than Lee at the time—where he was thirteen, she'd been fifteen. Did her children feel like she had?

Denise imagined their terror at the unknown. Would their mommy and daddy divorce? Would Mommy come home again? What would happen to them? Was this their fault?

Denise thought about her mom and how hard the abandonment had made life for her. Though she remarried after the divorce, the creeping sadness was a constant reminder that Denise's mom was a woman scorned. The replaying mantra "Like mother, like daughter" haunted Denise as she drove on.

And what of their future? Grandchildren not yet born?

Going to Grandpa's house then Grandma's house was not the same as going to Grandpa and Grandma's. Denise had seen the wear on her children because of her parents' split.

Denise's thoughts shifted to herself and a very different kind of concern. Dating.

"No way," she said to the empty car while streetlights flashed by. But an image of the new single guy at church popped into her mind. It would serve Sam right for her to date someone else, especially someone nice looking, just a shade younger. Let him see how it feels.

She shook her head and argued out loud with herself. "Get a grip. You're not single."

"Sam cheated. So you're free to explore the possibilities.

"But we're still married."

Tired of her own chatter, Denise stopped talking and turned the radio on. A favorite talk show was playing. Maybe a voice of wisdom coming through the speakers would offer clarity to her situation. She turned the volume up.

"First Corinthians 7:13–16 says that if a Christian woman has a husband who is not a believer and he is willing to continue living with her, she must not leave him. But if the husband or wife who isn't a believer insists on leaving, let them go. In such cases, the Christian husband or wife is no longer bound to the other, for God has called you to live in peace. Don't you wives realize that your husbands might be saved because of you? And don't you husbands realize that your wives might be saved because of you?" The radio host cleared his throat. "I think God is speaking to someone tonight. Is it you? If you're thinking of leaving your spouse, won't you first consider what God says about marriage?"

Denise snapped the radio off then pulled into a convenience store. She needed a drink.

After putting the lid on her bubbling cup of Coke, Denise walked to the register. While the attendant rang up her soda, she glanced at a row of cooler cups lining a shelf near the window. A purple one with pink script caught her eye: "I know God won't give me more than I can handle. I just wish He didn't trust me so much."

"You got that right."

"Excuse me?" The cashier's eyebrows knitted in confusion.

"Sorry. It's nothing. But I'll take this." She pulled the cup off the shelf and set it on the counter.

"Is that it?"

"Yes, thank you." Denise paid her bill, picked up her purchases, and got back in the car. Continuing her drive with no destination in mind, Denise crossed unnoticed miles in silence, troubling thoughts her only company.

Rays of coral streaked across the predawn sky when she wearily parked the car. The house was dark. Appeared quiet. She had driven full circle.

Denise bowed her head on the steering wheel and prayed, "Lord, grant me the serenity to accept the things I cannot change. The courage to change the things I can. And the wisdom to know the difference. In Jesus' name, amen." Then she steeled herself for what was to come and walked with determination back into her home.

For Sam and Denise, recovery took years. The road was often rough, but with much effort their relationship was restored. Sam showed deep remorse, took responsibility for his actions, and did his best to demonstrate genuine repentance.

A close friend wisely advised Denise to study the stages of grief early in the process, empowering her to recognize and accept the normalcy of her volatile emotional outbursts or depressive states of dark sadness. She cycled through love, hate, and numbness.

One night, alone in her bathtub, Denise cried out to God. "Teach me to love my husband again. Purify our marriage bed. Teach me to forgive what I truly don't want to forgive."

There were many close calls, where one or both nearly gave up on their marriage. For several months, Denise packed her suitcases, placed them in the closet, and lived out of them. In case God decided to release her from her marriage. It never happened.

Through it all, both husband and wife resolved to make love an action verb instead of hoping for warm, fuzzy noun feelings. They acted out intimacy—no matter how they felt, and it often didn't feel good.

They tried three different counselors before finding a pastor who helped them. He didn't berate Sam for his sin, but he didn't sugarcoat it either. He encouraged a compassionate and generous response to Denise's pain. He taught Sam to hold his wife and let her vent when she screamed, cried, and pummeled his chest. He showed Sam the scriptures where a husband is told to love his wife as Christ loves the church.

For Denise, the gentle pastor guided her to the books of Job and Hosea, where she found comfort in knowing she wasn't alone in the depth of her anguish. Ultimately, one assignment in particular changed her perspective, their marriage, and her life.

At this stage, Denise's nerves caused her to vomit numerous times a day. She wasn't sleeping well and she'd lost several pounds.

At the end of one weekly session, the pastor said, "Starting tonight, I want you to study your Bible with fresh eyes. I want you to look for anything new about Jesus you've never noticed before. Go on a quest to discover nuances in His character. Write them down."

Denise wasn't sure how this was going to help her marriage. But when she got home, she asked for divine help and decided to give it a try.

Her Bible crackled, and the smell of faux leather tickled her nose as she randomly swung the cover back. When the tissue pages settled, Isaiah 54:4 started at the top left. In wonder, Denise read out loud through verse 6: " 'Fear not; you will no longer live in shame. Don't be afraid; there is no more disgrace for you. You will no longer remember the shame of your youth and the sorrows of widowhood. For your Creator will be your husband; the LORD of Heaven's Armies is his name! He is your Redeemer, the Holy One of Israel, the God of all the earth. For the LORD has called you back from your grief—as though you were a young wife abandoned by her husband,' says your God" (NLT).

A strange thought tickled Denise's brain. She picked up a pen and started writing.

What if you were preparing as the bride of Christ for your marriage tomorrow? What qualities in Him as your future husband would you be grateful for?

She started listing general statements.

He forgives me. He died for me. He loves me.

But the more she focused on looking at Him with fresh eyes, the more personal her notes became.

Nothing I say is unimportant to Him. He listens no matter what time of day or night it is. He's never too tired to talk. He doesn't think I'm too emotional. He thinks I'm beautiful just the way He created me. He even likes me in my ugliest, oldest sweats. He's never unfaithful, and He definitely won't leave me. He understands what it feels like for the person you love the most to betray you. I do it to Him every day, and yet He stands by my side.

The list grew from there, but that night a miracle happened. Denise felt released from her fears of not being good enough. She no longer needed to pressure Sam for love. She realized she already had the perfect husband in Jesus Christ. There was nothing she could do to make Him love her any more or less than He already did. She was free to love Sam, mistakes and all. Wasn't that how Christ treated her?

Shortly after Denise's epiphany, another miracle happened. Sam finally grasped how badly he'd hurt her. She had prayed, asking God to let Sam know her pain without her having to do what he had done.

The answer came through a strange and ordinary event. One of Denise's male coworkers dropped a file off at their house, and Sam answered the door. Something sparked, and that night he cried in his wife's arms. Reality had set in, and he knew how close he had come to losing her. This was Sam's new beginning.

The dark valley of adultery is long behind them. Both husband and wife experienced many post-traumatic symptoms that nearly destroyed their marriage. But when their two grandchildren visit today and the family laughs around a board game, Sam squeezes Denise's hand, and they smile knowingly.

The tears, the screaming matches, the counseling, and the Bible study to see how God said a husband and wife should behave were all worth it. Early on they both decided to act in love until the feelings followed. In sickness and in health, for richer or for poorer, for better or for worse, they are standing strong. Denise and Sam discovered a secret to getting through the trauma of his infidelity. They looked to God—the creator of marriage—for guidance, realizing it doesn't take two to make things work; it takes three.

As you read this, you may wonder if your marriage is doomed because of adultery. Don't try to manipulate the outcome or play games. Attempts to make him/her jealous often backfire. Sympathy statements, playing the martyr, or other ploys wear thin in a short amount of time. A cheating spouse's pity for your tears quickly turns to hostility. Genuine emotions do not require exaggeration.

Decide in advance you will thrive whether your spouse stays or leaves. In the case of infidelity, the Bible says you can get a divorce. But just because you can doesn't mean you should. As much as it depends on you, give it all you've got. If things still don't work out, you can live with a clear conscience.

Don't get discouraged when a good day is followed by a bad week. Over time you'll begin to experience more moments that glow with hope. They will start lasting longer, until woven together, whole days glimmer with possibility. Your aches will subside. Someday you may find yourself supporting others, reaching back your hand to draw them through the darkness you've crawled out of.

I believe, like Denise, whether your marriage lasts past the affair or not, *you* will make it. You don't need a perfect spouse—you're in a relationship with a flawless partner.

The One who won't betray you, the One you can truly trust, the Bridegroom is waiting. He adores you. Accept His affection. Ask Him to forgive your unfaithfulness. Dance in His arms. And let Him love you as if you'd never been hurt. This is the great romance you've searched for since the day you were born.

Adultery is a crushing blow like other sudden and uncontrollable events. In an instant we're blindsided—like the true story in the following chapter. In the face of tragedy, we are sometimes taken to the edge of death.

Insider Insights

Emotional Healing

- Listen to the song "Restore" by Chris August. Whether your earthly marriage thrives or not, your love relationship with Jesus Christ proves you are desirable, beautiful, and wanted. Even if things look bleak, remember God is still in the miracle business.

- Manifest your emotions in poetry, dance, photography, song, or painting. Any creative expression can be used as a filter to get what's inside outside through a healthy outlet.

- Decide to forgive. Choose it before you feel it. Hebrews 11 describes faith—believe in restoration you cannot yet see. Transform the way you view your spouse and yourself by speaking well behind their back, whether they stay or leave.

Practical Help

- Reconciliation requires intention to keep your sexual intimacy fresh. Play the board game Monogamy: A Hot Affair. . .with Your Partner. Read books like *Red-Hot Monogamy: Making Your Marriage Sizzle* by Bill and Pam Farrel, *Sexperiment: 7 Days to Lasting Intimacy with Your Spouse* by Ed and Lisa Young, and *Sheet Music: Uncovering the Secrets of Sexual Intimacy in Marriage* by Dr. Kevin Leman.

- Familiarize yourself with the stages of grief (see www.recover-from-grief.com/7-stages-of-grief.html). The death of your marriage, as you knew it, may require a mourning process.

  1. Shock and denial
  2. Pain and guilt
  3. Anger and bargaining
  4. Depression, reflection, loneliness
  5. The Upward Turn
  6. Reconstruction and working through
  7. Acceptance and hope

- If your spouse leaves you, make a list and start checking things off one at a time:
  - Give yourself permission to do one thing you wanted to do, but your mate prevented in the past.
  - Start exercising immediately. Walking, running, aerobic dance, swimming, anything that gets your body moving and your endorphins releasing.
  - Vent your feelings by writing letters

to your spouse, the marital intruder, to God. Keep them private though, and destroy them when you're ready. There's nothing worse than publicly humiliating yourself with emotional outbursts you can't take back, especially in the permanency of social media or other online platforms. Your future self will thank you.

- Read something inspiring, encouraging, or funny.
- Develop an updated financial plan.
- Start a Gratitude Journal. Every day write down a minimum of three things you are thankful for. Nothing's too small or big.
- Add your own positive, simple, energizing activities to this list.

Spiritual Comfort

- Do you know your tears are so important to God that He saves them? He keeps track of all your sorrows (see Psalm 56:8). Let this healing knowledge wash over you with medicinal strength.
- "For your Maker is your husband—the LORD Almighty is his name—the Holy One of Israel is your Redeemer; he is called the God of all the earth" (Isaiah 54:5).
- Those who are forgiven much love much (see Luke 7:47). The greater your willingness to forgive the sins committed against you, the greater capacity there is for deep relationships in your future.

GUIDED PRAYER

Dear Jesus,

Thank You for being my bridegroom. I am captivated by Your commitment to show me what love is supposed to look like. I'm grateful You promised Your heart to me, and I promise mine to You.

CHAPTER 9

Crushing Blows

Imagine waking up every day with throbbing torment and no relief. Most of us can't relate. But how frustrating for those who appear fine on the outside yet are suffering on the inside.

One of my friends posted on Facebook this morning: "I honestly apologize to those with daily aches and pains. A few short months ago I didn't know my life would be turned upside down with such overconsuming pain that nothing seems to help. I just can't take it. Again, I am truly sorry."

My friend expressed sentiments similar to those I've heard from many who are facing traumatic episodes—people like Carla, who persists through something very hard to get through.

Carla wasn't scheduled to work when it happened. If only she hadn't covered the half-day rotation on someone else's Saturday. If only she would have waited. An extra thirty minutes before or after may have saved her years of agony. If only she would have walked down a different aisle right before it was time for her to clock out. But there was no sense in questioning God about those things. No one could go back in time, and nothing would change her circumstances now.

There are many ironies in Carla's story. Less than

twenty minutes before she was scheduled to get off, the woman who rallied for safety at work was crushed when she couldn't move fast enough. Sandwiched between a machine and a heavy rack, her body drew into itself, nearly causing her shoulders to touch each other in a U-shape from the force of the impact.

Carla heard her own ribs break—*snap. . .snap. . . snap*—before she crumpled on the floor. Due to a punctured lung, she could hardly breathe. Her entire body flooded with heat, getting hotter, hotter, and hotter. She groaned in agony, desperate for relief. But help would not come quickly. Due to multiple car accidents in the area, it took nearly forty minutes for an ambulance to arrive from a neighboring town.

At the hospital, and through subsequent follow-ups, doctors determined Carla broke her left clavicle and three ribs, crushed both shoulders, tore both AC joints, smashed her jaw, and caused massive damage inside her left arm. From her abdomen up, there were few body parts the accident hadn't mangled.

Carla was hurt in 2008 and spent most of the next two years distraught. Not only was she grieving the loss of her body as she'd known it, but now she had to battle courts, judges, attorneys, and her previous employer to get the medical attention she desperately needed from a work-related accident. Due to delayed surgeries and other treatments, her recovery was lessened and lengthened.

In the secret space of her own dark thoughts, Carla, previously strong in heart and will, fought a persistent and too-attractive temptation to take her own life. Tired of the fight, she felt like giving up. The only thing stopping her was the thought of her husband and children. This wasn't the legacy she wanted to leave. But even those reasons sometimes didn't feel like enough.

Carla described it this way. "After the accident, I couldn't even garden anymore. I can't explain how it makes you feel when you aren't capable of doing things you looked forward to."

I thought about the things I take for granted.

Welling up, Carla continued, "I couldn't take care of my family like I had—even the smallest things were impossible. On a good day, I could fold three towels. My husband and I built our house together, side by side, but a nice building, pretty furnishings, and special knickknacks no longer mattered. I felt like a prisoner in my own home."

She exhaled.

"While attorneys, doctors, insurance reps, and bill collectors bickered over *my* life, time slipped away. As the pain worsened, so did my family's finances. I lost my job because I couldn't work anymore."

I shook my head, unable to comprehend.

"At one point, I was so discouraged I went as far as making out my will. My husband didn't even know. I put the letter laying out my wishes in our safe. Then I went outside to walk, to think, and to rail at God. I looked up at the sky and said, 'I don't know how much more you expect me to take. I need a sign.' "

Carla's face softened, her eyes watered, and her voice cracked as she recalled the way God answered her unmasked request. With reverence in her tone, she recomposed herself and continued. "I was outside, and it felt like someone touched me on the shoulder. I glimpsed a flutter of white just behind my head. I didn't see it clearly, but it reminded me of a white dove. I thought a bird hit me. So I turned, looked around, but there was nothing there. I scanned the clouds, and nothing. But I knew. You might think I'm crazy, but I knew God had given me a sign. I just didn't know what it meant."

"I don't think you're crazy," I assured her.

She smiled through liquid-rimmed eyes. "I went inside and stood there for a few seconds trying to make sense of what happened. Then I went back outside and looked at the sky again, but there was nothing there. I'm telling you, though, I know something touched me—told me to wait. When I went back inside the second time, there was a message on my phone. Our new pastor had called to introduce himself. His recording said, 'When can we get together and talk?' I needed that call."

"And you needed that touch."

"Yeah. I did. Otherwise I might never have heard the message. When I called the pastor back, he wanted to get with me the next week, but I told him, 'I need to do it now.'"

Carla blinked several times before continuing. "If God hadn't tapped me on the shoulder and if the pastor hadn't called that day, I might not be here. When we met the first time, I told him everything. After that we talked many times. He walked me through the delays in treatment, the frustrations with the doctors and lawyers, and then—the other news."

I thought how Carla, deprived of productivity, independence, and a pain-free life, fought the siren call of suicide. Believing death better than the torture, she had contemplated various ways to die. But one possibility hadn't crossed her mind until the uncontrollable forced it on her.

After the accident, Carla was so swollen, it affected her ability to breathe. Tests revealed there was more to her bulging neck than the calamity implied. Her thyroid was removed with the doctor's assurance, "It's not cancer." But he was wrong.

The biopsy came back positive. And Carla had a new epiphany.

The look of resolve on her face matched the strength in her voice when she told me this part of her story. "It made me realize how much I *didn't* want to take my life. It put a twist on how I felt about things. While I was feeling sorry for myself, I realized I might not make it now, but not by my choice. When I got the diagnosis, I realized I wasn't ready to go."

I touched Carla's arm to show my compassion. "So cancer was your wake-up call."

"Yep. This hit me from left field. It may sound strange, but my cancer was a godsend. It made me realize how much I wanted to fight for my life, even though it's not easy. I discovered I didn't have control over my death; God did. But I also realized my own desperation to live. I wasn't ready to check out after all."

Before me sat a woman who displayed more than a desire to be alive—she demonstrated a renewed will to *live* alive. Regardless of what was handed to her.

She continued. "One thing that surprised me from going through all of this was remembering a friend from long before the accident. I'd spoken to him two days before he killed himself. He had a five-month-old baby and a wife with breast cancer. At the time, I got mad. I thought, *How dare he act so selfishly?*

"Now I realize I could have done the same thing. I was a strong person before the accident. I never dreamed I would consider suicide, but now I know how it feels to reach that point. I have a better understanding of the desperation he must have fought right before he died. It's a caution for those who don't think it could happen to them—none of us are immune to complete despair if things get bad enough."

I pictured Carla standing before the coffin of her friend. Shaking her head as she contemplated what his wife and baby would face without him. Knowing how thin the line is to something you can never take back.

Carla's voice pulled me from my thoughts. "One of the things that continues to help me is venting to God. When the stabs in my arm are so bad that I literally want to saw it off, I let Him know how I feel." She rubbed her shoulder habitually. "Have you seen the movie *Soul Surfer*?"

"Yes."

"I feel the pain of that girl every time I watch the movie. Sometimes I wish I'd lost my arm. I wonder if it would be easier because I wouldn't have this chronic pain from compressed nerves the doctors can't do anything about. But it's comforting to realize God understands what I'm going through. He knows exactly what I'm talking about. And I need that, because even the people closest to me can't grasp how much I deal with."

Thinking about the wisdom of her statement, I said, "Unless we experience something, you're right, we don't get it. I know if someone complains of a bellyache, I don't appreciate how bad they really feel unless I've had one recently myself. Especially if they don't look that sick on the outside."

Carla's eyes lit up with excitement. "Exactly. Because I look okay on the surface and I fight hard to live as normally as I can, people don't understand how much pain I'm in."

"Has it been hard on your relationships?"

"The thing I'm challenged with most is letting go of what I can't do, because I've always been the doer. I've come to realize I'll never be the person I was before. When you can't even lift your arms above your head, it's hard."

I grimaced. "How awful for you."

"I'm finally coming to a place where I'm starting to accept my situation." She twisted a piece of paper around her finger. "These days my family struggles with it more than I do. Because he lives with me, my husband is starting to get it and doesn't pressure me as much. But the rest of my family doesn't understand I'm not the same person. I'll never be able to do all the things I did before. They still want me to fix things for them, but I can't. These days I don't even offer advice. I tell them, 'Don't ask me what I think. Ask God what He wants you to do.'"

"Wise words."

"I've learned from losing pretty much everything that I don't know nearly as much as I thought I did."

"The older we get, the less we know, right?" We both laughed in agreement.

A few seconds later, Carla's expression turned serious again. "Early on, we had to start selling our assets."

"I'm so sorry."

Carla shrugged. "When the lady who bought our horses asked why we were selling, I told her what happened. She asked me if I'd seen a counselor. I told her no but said I had talked with my pastor several times. She told me I needed to grieve what I'd lost. I didn't understand what she meant at first. After all, no one had died from the accident. But she explained that we mourn a lot of things, and I needed to grieve losing a fully functioning body. I really thought about it and realized she was right. I'm still grieving, especially as new things come up."

I nodded my head to urge her on.

"At my last appointment, the doctor didn't have

good news. He said, 'You've been crushed. We can only fix so much. There's nothing more we can do. You're just going to have to deal with it. You'll need physical therapy three or four days a week for the rest of your life.'

"When he told me that, I felt woozy and my mouth went dry. It's hard to swallow that even if I keep working hard, there's no guarantee I'll ever get better. At best, I may not go backward."

My stomach knotted at the thought of Carla hearing the finality of those words. "How do you plan to handle that?"

"My attorney asked if I wanted to get another opinion. At first I said no. I'm tired of the battle. As much as I hurt physically, fighting to get help is almost as traumatic."

Carla sighed. "Now that I've had more time to think, I might see what someone else has to say. If I would have listened to what I was first told, I wouldn't have gotten relief in my left shoulder down into my arm. The doctors have been wrong more than once."

Carla's faith makes her one tenacious woman.

Six years and five surgeries after the accident, there's not a single day when Carla is free from some form of searing, persistent physical pain. Her bones scrape against exposed nerves. Her pulled chest muscles refuse to mold back into form. Her limp left arm tugs with gravity, resculpting her posture in unnatural ways. Her right arm, attempting to compensate for the weakness in her left, is strained with a lingering soreness that rarely goes away. Her frame fatigues itself, battling a body determined to wear her down.

She describes one of her ongoing struggles like this: "Imagine someone constantly shoving a large knife into your elbow, never letting up—that's what it feels like. Working part-time is a grind, but it gives me purpose. It allows me to feel like I'm contributing to something bigger than myself."

In spite of her circumstances, Carla has a super-natural resolve to get through something she will never get over. She and her husband sold the home they built together in order to downsize for financial as well as practical reasons. She's no longer capable of maintaining space that size. You might think she feels sorry for herself, but the woman I sat with said she feels freed from the prison of "too much."

Carla told me her hardships had taught her one very powerful lesson—how to pray more effectively. Her statement reminded me of something I've learned from going through my own series of adversities. No matter what type of trauma I've endured, I've discovered there's a powerful formula to praying persuasively.

First, tap into the potency of thanking God in advance for good reports or outcomes. Philippians 4:6 tells us, "Do not be anxious about anything, but in every situation, by prayer and petition, *with thanksgiving*, present your requests to God" (emphasis added). Thank God before you see results. After all, according to Hebrews 11:1, faith is having confidence in the assurance of what we cannot yet see.

Second, don't miss the importance of confession and compounding your prayers with those of righteous partners. James 5:16 says, "Confess your sins to each other and pray for each other so that you may be healed. The prayer of a righteous person is powerful and effective."

Third, rightness with God means believing Him. Genesis 15:6 gives us the perfect example: "Abram believed the Lord, and he credited it to him as righteousness."

Fourth, connect with the chain-breaking force of praise. We only have to look at Acts 16:25–26 to see how singing tribute to God can set us free: "About midnight Paul and Silas were praying and singing hymns to God, and the other prisoners were listening to them. Suddenly there was such a violent earthquake that the foundations of the prison were shaken. At once all the prison doors flew open, and everyone's chains came loose." When you reach rock bottom, do what you least feel like—sing thanks to God and let Him free you from restricting pain.

Finally, allow God to be God. Trust Him, even when the results aren't what you hoped for. Remember: He sees the end from the beginning (see Isaiah 46:10). He knows unsearchable things you cannot know unless you call out to Him (see Jeremiah 33:3). His plans, though sometimes unclear at first, are to do us good and not harm (see Jeremiah 29:11–12). Our momentary struggles on earth are meant to equip us to help others and have meaning beyond what we initially see (see 2 Corinthians 1:4–5).

Blind trust is one of the most difficult things we are called to do, but it is the most powerful way to get through something you can't get over. There's an enigma in how faith works. Believing what you can't yet see is the secret key to unlocking the door to purpose-filled realities—no matter how much you hurt.

Carla has a realistic yet hope-filled view of living. This helps her move from self-condemnation so she can flourish in freedom.

I, too, share Carla's ambitious outlook. I learned this optimistic view the hard way—by staring death in the face. I invite you into a very private experience, in which I saw a supernatural miracle firsthand.

INSIDER INSIGHTS

Emotional Healing

- "Move" by MercyMe is a fight song for anyone experiencing ongoing battles against chronic pain or fatigue, regardless of its origin. Turn it on loud. Sing the words with gusto. And even if the only movement you are capable of is mental, dare to move your mind-set up and believe there will be brighter days ahead.

- Become intentional and schedule humor in your days, especially when you feel debilitated. Scripture says a cheerful heart is a medicine (see Proverbs 17:22), and science supports the healing power of laughter as well. Try to watch at least one funny movie a week, read a humorous book monthly, and get a daily dose of clean jokes at online sites like these: www.godslittleacre.net/funnies or jokes.ochristian.com. With whatever else ails you, don't let your funny bone break too.

- Take the focus off yourself temporarily. Carla says she watches the movie *The Passion of the Christ*, explaining that the scene of Jesus' beating reminds her that any pain she endures doesn't compare to His torture in sacrifice for our sins. Most of us can find examples of someone who has suffered from, or is going through, something more terrible than anything we've experienced.

Practical Help

- Let something go. Out of fear, we often hold on to material possessions far longer than we should when freedom awaits. If necessary, sell your home and downsize before your finances reach a breaking point. Get rid of pleasure items, especially those you can no longer enjoy. Any reduction in the amount of space you care for, or in possessions requiring ongoing maintenance, insurance, or taxes, minimizes your stress financially, mentally, and emotionally. One less thing for you to manage can reduce tomorrow's burdens and make things bearable.

- Refuse to accept a doomsday prognosis. Get second, third, fourth, or a dozen opinions from reputable professionals if needed. The world is full of people with inspiring stories because they refused to give up—regardless of what others said.
- Try to find at least one purpose-filled thing you can do. A reason to get out of bed each morning. Something beyond yourself where you can contribute to a greater good. A smile or encouraging word to someone else is a great start.

Spiritual Comfort
- When things fall apart, we assume something bad happened because we did something wrong, making God angry with us. But in fact, a difficulty is often a miracle in the making, simply so God is seen and glorified (see John 9:1–5).
- It is through the storms of life that God speaks, showing us power, wisdom, and provision (see Job 38:1–41).
- Pray aloud, with sincerity and thanksgiving, your desire for God to rescue you for His name's sake, so all the nations and kingdoms of the earth will know He alone is Lord (see 2 Kings 19:19).

GUIDED PRAYER

Dear God,

I don't understand why I'm going through this. But I stand on Your promises, in faith, believing for what I don't yet see or feel. Like Abraham, Job, Isaiah, Jeremiah, and others in the Bible, I will continue to strive each day to move in whatever direction You give me strength, guidance, and energy for. Thank You for not leaving me or forsaking me. Thank You for understanding when I need to take the mask off and rail in raw and honest ways. Thank You for small signs, encouragements, and surprise reminders of Your presence, for taps on the shoulder. Jesus, thank You that I'm not going through anything You haven't experienced Yourself.

CHAPTER 10

Scars of Love

I've done this, and I can't take it back.

On May 19, 1997, this was my first coherent thought upon waking—sheer panic. I squinted and blinked at the bright white lights in the ICU recovery room. A woman seemed to speak through a muffled tunnel. "Anita? Are you with us?"

I think I nodded yes.

I closed my eyes against the harsh white, not quite ready to face what I'd just done. I took a burning breath of sanitized air, feeling the chemicals wash my nostrils and throat with germ-killing efficiency. I shifted on the bed. A sharp sting stabbed the deep tissues of my left side. My eyes popped open in surprise, allowing the sterile room decor to temporarily blind me.

"Lie still and rest," the muffled voice said while patting my arm with a soothing touch.

Something in the way she talked reminded me of my mom. I closed my eyes again and swallowed the thick metallic spittle forming on my tongue. I was grateful for her maternal permission to relax my weary eyes.

The sweet faces of my two young sons wafted into my mind's view. As I had done so many times during the previous months, I reviewed the concerns I'd had prior to the surgery. What if one of my boys needs a kidney in the future and I can't give them one? What if my remaining kidney contracts a disease or quits functioning?

The chilly hospital sheet covering my body caused goose bumps to raise on my arms. The cold brought my thoughts back to the present. *What had I done?* But I knew it was too late to change my mind now.

Then I thought of my sister. I remembered receiving the letter from her doctor saying, "She will need a transplant."

There was no question; I would try to donate.

The decision wasn't easy. It put stress on my marriage as my husband and I both wrestled with our fears. But in my mind, this wasn't about me. This was about my sister, whom I loved very much.

Now that the surgery was over, it didn't matter what anyone thought, including me. And a new issue was vying for my attention. I was starting to feel the fire from the doctor's scalpel where he'd opened up my whole left side. Thankfully, narcotics soon flowed into my spine via epidural, and I drifted back into a drug-induced sleep. I missed most of Monday.

I spent much of Tuesday trying not to move, sneeze, or laugh. I was mostly successful—when I was awake.

On Wednesday, however, things changed. The doctor came in and said, "We need to remove the epidural today."

Something came over me when I heard those words. I immediately felt like I was ten years old, had fallen off my bike, and had the air knocked out of my lungs, wondering if I'd breathe freely again.

Blind terror crept into my gut. "Do you have to take it out?" I pleaded.

"We can't leave the epidural in, but we'll put you on Dilaudid, a morphine derivative for your pain."

"Can you wait one more day?"

A look of compassion spread over the attractive middle-aged doctor's face. He took a few steps closer and shook his head no. "Don't worry, we'll take good care of you."

Further begging was futile, so I sniffled, "All right."

"Good." And with that, he scribbled on my medical chart before striding out of the room.

It started within minutes of the change. Something didn't feel right. By that evening, my feeling intensified.

A smothering sensation covered my nose and mouth. Even though I was breathing, I wasn't getting air. My tongue seemed three times larger than normal. And a burning started on my upper lip, extending diagonally toward my left cheek. By bedtime, I knew if I fell asleep I wouldn't wake up.

The nurse came in to check my vitals. She tugged on the blood pressure cuff, and it loosened with a crackle of Velcro. "109 over 68," she chirped.

"I feel strange." I noticed the rasp in my own voice.

"What's wrong, hon?" Concern crossed her features as she tossed a rebellious strand of blond out of her blue eyes.

"My tongue is blocking my throat."

"Dilaudid can make you feel that way."

"Having trouble getting air."

"Let's check your oxygen." She placed a probe over my finger. "You're a little low. Nothing to be overly concerned about—we can take care of it." She smiled sympathetically then slid two-pronged tubes up my nostrils. They were connected to an oxygen tank.

Cool air swept through my nasal passages, and relief flooded my veins.

"Better?"

"Yes. Thank you."

"Now get some rest."

I nodded but knew sleep was out of the question. The foreboding sense I'd never wake up was more powerful than my desire to rest.

The clock was not my friend. *Tick. . .tick. . .tick.* I glanced at the big numbers, pointy hands, and round black frame on the wall. A mere minute had passed, though it felt like an hour. It was going to be a very long night. My body ached from fatigue.

By 11:00 p.m., I could feel my eyelids betraying me. Sleep was not an option, but the bed was not helping. I made a hard decision.

Going against every instinct to avoid the pain in my side, I prepared myself.

I slipped the tubes over my head and laid them on the pillow. Like taking a big gulp of air before plunging into water, I pulled a big breath of cool oxygen into my lungs through my nose. Then I gripped the IV pole. With a loud grunt, I heaved the dead weight of my body away from the bed. Sweat caused my palm to slip. A fiery sword stabbed my side.

I quickly grabbed a bit higher and let my hand suction against the metal, strengthening my hold. Halfway into a seated position, I stopped.

"Hee, hee, who," I panted into the pain. "Hee, hee, who." The huffing sharpened my focus and relaxed my muscles, giving me enough strength to tug again. The agony intensified as I cautiously swung my legs over the edge of the bed. I made it into a hunched standing position. Fire singed the insides of my left abdomen and across my back. For a moment, I thought my knees would buckle. But after more labored breathing, I gripped the IV pole tighter then scuffed my feet, taking my first tiny steps since presurgery on Monday.

When I finally got to the doorway, I looked back at the big clock. Nearly twenty minutes to walk three or four feet. My body was wringing with cold sweat, and I felt like I'd run, swum, and biked an Ironman. But my determination to stay awake overshadowed my weariness. I was not ready to die.

Once momentum kicked in, the first lap wasn't too bad. I learned how to time my breathing with steps least likely to send shooting burns around the core of my body. It took me an hour and a half to circle the nurse's station, arriving back at my room just before 1:00 a.m.

I shuffled to the water pitcher on my hospital tray, poured to the top of the clear plastic cup next to it, and guzzled the refreshing drink. Then I snatched some tissues and wiped my soaked forehead and face before swigging another full cup of water. With my parched throat quenched, I was ready to go again.

My speed increased on the next circle. When I approached the nurse's station, a familiar sweet smile greeted me. She picked up a chart nearby, scanned the page, then said, "Wow, look at you. Feeling all right?"

Not willing to confess the swell of alarm rattling my insides, I worked up a weak smile and rasped, "Good."

"It's almost time to check your vitals. I guess we can do it right here. Okay with you?"

I nodded agreement.

The nurse placed the thermometer in my mouth and the blood pressure cuff on my arm. Several seconds later, she announced, "Temp's good. 99.2. Your blood pressure's come down a bit, but still in a healthy range. 104 over 68. I'd say you're doing great."

I sure didn't feel great.

"Let me know if you need anything."

I nodded my response to her and started scooting my feet in rhythmic scuffs again, afraid more talking would expose the truth of how I really felt.

The hospital corridor felt massive on the next journey around. After I drank another cup of water, I glanced at the bed. It was looking more inviting now that it was two thirty in the morning. But I pressed on.

During my fourth lap, I slowed substantially. It took me almost two hours. Exhaustion was now stronger than my fear. It was nearly six thirty when I yelped, collapsing in the bed. At this point, I was still terrified, but willing to make my peace with God and ready to submit to whatever waited for me on the other side of death.

But I didn't get the chance to say more than a brief prayer. The fall onto the bed caused pain to radiate around my side—it consumed my thoughts and snapped me awake. Frozen in place, all I could think was, *Don't move.* And I didn't.

It took awhile for the throbbing to ease and my nerves to calm. Both finally did. But if sleep thought it was going to sneak in and get the upper hand, a new nurse who came to take my vitals had another idea.

"How are we this morning?" Her chipper tone grated against my tired and sickly disposition.

"I've felt better." My voice sounded gruff, but in a weak sort of way, as if I were speaking through a watery hollow.

She strapped Velcro in place around my arm, setting the blood pressure cuff to automatically squeeze and measure, then focused her attention on my eyes. "What do you mean you've felt better?"

I inhaled as best I could. "Feel weird. Breathing, but like nothing's coming in." As if needing to demonstrate, I had to interrupt myself to pull more air into my lungs. "Afraid to sleep."

The nurse rubbed my upper arm. "Oh honey, you need your sleep so your body can recover." She tugged at the cuff. "101 over 62." She used her finger as a pointer, reading the chart she'd brought with her. "Both numbers have dropped some. We'll keep an eye on it. Let me check your oxygen." Her eyebrows crinkled. "It's down too. I know you've been walking, which is good, but you need to keep this on whenever you're in your bed. Nurse's orders." She gently slipped the clear tubes back over my head, easing each vent into a nostril so fresh oxygen could infiltrate my system.

The slight whoosh of air did make me feel a bit better, and I even closed my eyes, allowing the tension to ease.

The nurse spoke in a soothing tone, "That's it. A nap will do you good."

Her words caused my eyes to fly open. I wanted to tell her a nap might kill me. But her back was already turned as she exited the room, and I didn't have the strength to yell. So I lay there, in a pool of adrenaline, my terror keeping me awake.

Soon after, my mom came in, so under her watchful care I spent the day trying to catnap. Yet I couldn't shake the slow and steady sense that my body was shutting down. Every few hours when my vitals were taken, the numbers dropped a little more, but subtly, so the medical staff was alert but not panicked.

By evening, I could barely talk above a hoarse whisper. If someone asked me a question, I tried to nod or use facial expressions to answer.

My mother-in-law called so I could speak to my children, but I only had the energy to wave the phone off when my mom offered it. It broke my heart, but I had no strength—even for the ones who meant the most to me on earth.

I didn't move much, conserving what little energy

I had left, while inside my thoughts never stopped. An onslaught of mental attacks kept my mind pumped. A blessing and a curse. They kept me awake so I didn't slip into a never-ending sleep, but the panic I felt over the dying process was like a presence in the room.

It's hard to explain how it feels to gasp for breath, feeling the rhythm of air going in and out of your lungs but knowing it isn't transferring into your blood, your organs, or your cells. Feeling your body let go.

When visiting hours ended and I was left alone again, I spoke honestly and silently to God through my thoughts. *If You exist, please forgive me for all of the things I've done wrong. For my selfish ways. For acting like I didn't need You. Because if You are there, I do need You, and though I don't deserve it, I'm asking for another chance. I'm asking to get to know You if You are willing to show me who You are. Amen.*

Then I forced myself out of bed and pulled another all-nighter. Circling the nurse's station, avoiding eye contact and conversation, clinging to the IV pole during waves of blackening fogs, hoping I wouldn't pass out.

The small hand of the big black clock was on the five and the large hand on the four when I shuffled back into my room for the last time. As scared as I was of dying, I could push myself no more. It was almost five thirty on Friday morning, four days after the kidney transplant, and as I lay there contemplating how it was going to feel to die, she stepped into the doorway.

My sister.

We hadn't seen each other since right before the surgery. At that time, donors and recipients weren't allowed to share rooms post-transplant in case of organ rejection. But that was seventeen years ago. A lot has changed since then.

As a living donor advocate, today I strive to raise awareness of the emotional needs for those who will walk the hard but satisfying valley leading to the gift of life. And so events such as what happened to me won't happen to someone else.

Because in 1997, when my sister entered my Denver hospital room, I was near death—and I knew it.

"How are you doing?" She tiptoed in.

I could only rasp out the words. "Scared. I brought a Bible. In the bag." I raised my left hand a couple inches off the bed and pointed toward the floor. "Can you get it?"

Prior to the surgery, I wasn't a Bible reader; I didn't believe it was the inspired Word of God. How could we trust that what it said today hadn't been distorted over time and terrain? But of course I'd never read it for myself either. Back then I made a lot of uninformed decisions about something I didn't know much about.

But my mom had given me a Bible for my sixteenth birthday. So when I left my home in Missouri for the trip to Denver, I dusted off the white leather cover and tossed it in a book bag, not knowing how desperately I would cling to it later.

Now, as my breathing became increasingly labored and my bodily functions weakened, I was desperate for anything that might save my life, or more importantly, might save my soul. In case God was real, I hoped holding on to the Bible would prove enough to pacify Him as I left Earth and entered the unknown. But my sister didn't hand it to me.

Instead, she offered, "Would you like me to read you something?"

I nodded yes.

"What do you want to hear?"

"Don't care."

To this day I can't tell you where she read from. But within seconds, the room changed. Her voice dimmed. I could hear the ebb and flow of her words, but I wasn't listening. My attention was drawn to something else.

Like someone opening the curtains on a big stage, a thin veil pulled back, revealing a reality more vibrant than anything I'd experienced before. Though my body was lying in bed, unmoved, I was transported into another world.

A flash of yellow light passed in front of me. Another came from the opposite side. Then I noticed they were flying in all different directions. I concentrated on making out what they were, but it was hard because they moved so fast. Like bolts of yellow lightning. Finally, I saw their source—large flaming swords carried by beings without clear form, illuminated in a softer white glow. But they weren't alone.

To my left, a large face with an evil, distorted expression came close. I sensed danger. Then just before its gnarled claws reached me, a flash of light knocked it back. I couldn't see mouths move, and there was no sound in my ears, but I could hear them argue all the same.

"Let me have her."

"She does not belong to you."

"She's mine."

"She is not yours to take."

Back and forth they wrangled, words clashing as they fought. They were battling for my soul. As terrifying as that knowledge was, what scared me most was not knowing who would win.

I had no concept of time while I watched. But at some point, I heard my sister calling my name. In an instant, the veil closed, and I was back in the hospital room.

Now before I go any further, let me address the skeptics. I am a pretty balanced person in my thinking, both logical and emotional. I am not prone to dreams and visions nor delusional outbursts, and I don't see demons around every corner. If someone else told me this story, I would wonder if they were exaggerating or telling an out-and-out lie. But it isn't someone else's story—it's mine.

In a Denver hospital, I glimpsed a supernatural world with invisible forces at work behind the scenes of my life. Call it a vision, a near-death experience, a reaction to the meds, whatever you like, but I know it was reality. Truer and more powerful than anything I've experienced before or since. It was also private. My sister neither heard nor saw any of it.

What she did see was that something was wrong. She called our mother at the hotel where she was staying nearby. Within minutes, the room buzzed with doctors and nurses. When they checked my vital signs, everything was lethally low.

They immediately took me off Dilaudid and put me on another pain med. Within minutes I could tell the difference. Two hours later, with my mother's assistance, I was able to take my first shower. By the afternoon, I could talk again.

But I was no longer the same person who entered the hospital on Monday.

I had prayed for God's forgiveness, with no time to worry about doing it right. My concern was in doing it honestly. And though more struggles awaited in my immediate future, I no longer felt alone.

Three weeks passed before I finally returned home so my body could heal. With time at my disposal, I decided to read through the entire Bible, determined to make an informed decision about its contents. It took me a few months, but when I closed the cover after reading the last word, I knew.

There was no individual or group of people who had wisdom and insight required to speak to the millennia of humans before Christ as well as to twenty-first-century people after His death. I finally understood why some referred to the Bible as the living Word of God. The concepts, principles, and truths don't die; they continue to comfort, teach, and encourage. For those who question whether God is real, the Bible is where you can hear His voice offering hope and joy, spoken personally to us through His letters of love.

During that time, I learned why I needed to read the Bible for myself instead of trusting what someone else said about it. I saw the importance of consistency, spending at least fifteen minutes a day reading the Bible, whether I felt like it or not.

I now know that when I don't feel like it is when I unearth some of the most thrilling help.

The aftereffects of the transplant, as well as almost dying from my allergic reaction to Dilaudid, left me with powerful post-traumatic symptoms. For nearly three months after the surgery, I hardly slept. When I did doze, I'd quickly wake, bolting upright with sweat pouring off my chin, flashbacks taking me back to the time when I couldn't get enough oxygen.

I feared death to the point I was afraid of leaving my house and hyperventilated at the thought of riding in a car. Soon I slipped deep into the pit of my first bout with clinical depression. I no longer led my life—PTSD led me.

That was then—a temporary yet agonizing season of my life. But after putting one foot in front of the other, refusing to stop, today my life is flooded with light.

I learned a lot through my experience as a living donor, much of it difficult. But I want to be clear: if given the chance, knowing what I do now, I'd jump at the chance to do it again. For one, technology and patient awareness has improved dramatically over the past seventeen years and continues to do so.

Second, I've found much purpose in my pain. Today I'm a living donor advocate. Had I not walked the dark valley of near death, I would not have a heart of compassion for those who are hurting. I would not be writing this book. Most importantly, I couldn't share how faith in God can carry you through something you will never get over.

My kidney can never return to my body. In actuality, it is no longer mine. It belongs to my sister. It is hers to do with as she wishes. However, my remaining kidney has adjusted. Now it processes an equivalent of two-thirds what both kidneys took care of together. Seventeen years later, I am healthier than most people my age. I am aware I need to take mild precautions, but am unwilling to stop living my life. I travel, explore, give, dare, and occasionally indulge.

Because of my close relationship with Jesus Christ, I can also speak authentically about peace, joy, love, and happiness. I have found no other way to make it through the valleys than to grab hold of His hand. He leads me out of the darkness. He is my way, my truth, and my life.

No matter what your circumstances, I urge you to keep going. If God cares about the lilies of the field and the birds in the sky, which He does, then dare to believe, dare to trust, that His unfailing love can carry you through whatever it is you can't get over. Accept His outstretched hand.

And yet, though God is always with us, there is

a loss that feels unbearable, a passage of catastrophic magnitude, a journey every mother begs not to tread. In the next chapter, we'll address something no one wants to face—the tragedy of death's destructive path.

INSIDER INSIGHTS

Emotional Healing

- When confronted with your own mortality, or the helpless inability to control your life, "Take You Back" by Jeremy Camp offers renewed hope, strength, and power to help you through things you don't immediately understand.

- Living donors commonly experience grief over the loss of their organs. As one physician described it to me, "Much like mourning the loss of a parent, a spouse, or a child, you are mourning the loss of your body part. A piece of you is now gone." Whatever you've lost, give yourself permission to go through all the necessary parts of the healing process.

- I learned to accept and embrace my emotional side because of my post-traumatic stress after facing death. I have a better understanding of my God-given feelings, created in His image, and I don't need to apologize for having them. Stuffing our emotions is unhealthy; expressing them is healing.

Practical Help

- Give thanks for things you've previously taken for granted. Walking to the bathroom alone. Hot showers. A healthy appetite. Ability to sleep. Sneezing or laughing without pain. Make your own list.

- When anxiety strikes, ask yourself, "What's the worst thing that could happen, and how likely is it?" A logical look at circumstances can help reduce traumatic symptoms.

- Aromatherapy provides a calming influence through smell. Carry a small bottle of your favorite soothing essential oil for a quick breeze of tranquility when you start to worry.

Spiritual Comfort

- When you recognize the onset of a panic attack, get your Bible out and start reading aloud. Speak passages like Psalm 27 as a song of gratitude.

- Why are we afraid to trust God today? Have we become so disillusioned (He said no or "not right now" when we wanted a yes right away), frightened (*Does He hate me? Is He mad at me? Will He do good things for other people but not me?*), or intimidated (*I don't want others to accuse me of believing ancient superstitions*) that we are now unwilling to show faith? Many say they believe in God, but how many *believe Him*? I'd rather believe, live a life of no regrets, and be wrong than risk unbelief only to find out there are no do-overs (see Psalm 78:21–22).

- Try the Bible if you never have. Jump back in if it's been a while. Keep on reading if you already do. There's power in its passages—the Word has been with God from the beginning and represents who He is today (see John 1:1). Don't take someone else's word for it nor discount it if you haven't investigated its pages. See for yourself whether there's anything to what the Bible says.

GUIDED PRAYER

Dear Jesus,

I agree with Job 13:15—though You slay me, yet will I place my hope and trust in You. Thank You for protecting me from myself and assuring me I can spend eternity in paradise with You because You've forgiven my past.

CHAPTER 11

Death's Destructive Path

Can anyone get over the loss of their own flesh and blood? I can't imagine a more traumatic experience than the death of your child. Although we somewhat expect some deaths, the sting isn't lessened when the final moment arrives. And some passings slam us in the gut with their illogical and unnatural stealth.

The grieving process shakes the faith of the strongest soul, but when you are unexpectedly deprived of another hug, another conversation, another kiss, another laugh with one who is part of you, nothing fills the void. Unresolved grief is a vicious enemy, stealing, killing, and destroying the lives of those who mourn.

Often, the agony of death parlays into long-lasting symptoms of PTSD in an otherwise normal life. In the case of a parent in unending sorrow, your old normal never returns again.

Post-traumatic stress disorder caused by any shocking event can make you feel as if you've lost your ability to function wholly as a human being. Even more so when your child dies. But in fact, you are not insane. You are exhibiting the signs of intense sorrow. PTSD is a natural reaction to abnormal stress.

Along with a sense of lunacy, other documented symptoms follow serious trauma. Sleep is often elusive.

Fits of rage shock the rager as well as those on the receiving end of an attack. Intense anxiety is common, especially if fear for another loved one is at stake. Withdrawals and sullenness can replace an outgoing and happy personality. An inability to talk about much of anything except the trauma often supersedes other conversations. Morbid doomsday thinking overshadows reflections of hope. Desperate attempts are made to regain control. This is normal for what you're going through.

When we mourn any tragic loss, post-traumatic stress blossoms in similar ways. We should expect to cope with some or all of the following:

- hypervigilance
- avoidance
- isolation
- extreme anxiety
- irritability
- inability to sleep
- nightmares
- flashbacks

Revisiting the tragedy in our minds and in our conversations provides a natural process of healing by which we force ourselves to face our pain rather than avoid it, stuff it, or try to run from it. Studies are now taking place in Little Rock, Arkansas, where the Department of Veterans Affairs (VA) is currently using prolonged exposure therapy to help soldiers returning from battle deal with their post-traumatic stress. By repeatedly guiding survivors through their torturous memories, therapists have proven the process is beneficial for many. The VA learned about prolonged exposure therapy from the positive results reported by victims of rape who had undergone this kind of therapy. Through their work, the VA has shown that other kinds of trauma also respond well to the treatment.[9]

In prolonged exposure therapy, every time survivors relive their painful event(s), they become stronger. When we continuously talk about our losses, we are essentially doing the same, only informally without a professional guide. I am not advising that you do this without counsel, but I am telling you that if you have an intrinsic need to keep talking about what happened to you, this can be a natural part of your healing.

Through her story here, a friend of mine is doing just that. She is a mother, wife, and grandmother currently stepping through a journey most of us can't imagine.

She was exploring Paris the day a mother's worst fears became reality. As Debby played Parisian tourist, her family in Moore, Oklahoma, hunkered down. How could she know while she laughed with her son, daughter-in-law, and grandchildren, a monster approached back home?

Debby did nothing wrong in those moments— actually she was doing something very right. She was doing what she was made for. Celebrating the art of God's creation. Learning from history. Savoring the landscape. While breathing the scents of Europe, she smiled and laughed, touching the hearts of her children and grandchildren. Debby was tasting life—something she would find difficult to continue in the ensuing weeks and months.

Called one of the worst tornadoes in American history, on Monday, May 20, 2013, the twister swept businesses, homes, schools, cars, and human lives into its murderous dust. The sky darkened as a massive steel-blue wall cloud, tinged in ghostly green, deepened its grip across the horizon. News agencies on television and radio implored the citizens skirting Oklahoma City's metropolitan and suburban areas to seek shelter immediately.

"Folks, this is not a tornado warning—it's a tornado emergency."

"Take cover underground. I repeat, get underground. Hiding in a shelter above ground could prove fatal."

"Do not get caught in your car. And do not hide under an overpass. The winds will accelerate and strengthen under bridges and highways."

On the tornado's approach, the cone developed quickly. It hurled missiles in the form of trees, rocks, bricks, lumber, broken windows, furniture, and cars out of its swirling sides. The stovepipe transformed into a mile-wide wedge. It clashed with electric poles and transformers, causing power flashes of white to momentarily illuminate its dark, hungry face. Massive flames shot up from multiple gas explosions, scorching the air with smoke.

Men, women, and children trembled as the massive funnel blasted across the earth, advancing toward heavily populated areas. The huge debris ball thickened in violent rotation. It set its track eastward and barreled closer to Debby's daughter, Jeany, leveling houses and churning through schools as it bore down.

Shortly after 3:00 p.m., when the Moore monster arrived at Sixth Street, it roared with deafening growls, lashing out with a furious temper. Children screamed, dogs barked, and birds silenced. Grown men and women stopped all activity. They moved away from windows, hid their families in storm cellars and interior safe rooms, under mattresses in bathtubs, and beneath stairwells.

Unchurched people prayed with faithful followers. Fervently. Desperately.

In an interior closet, thirty-eight-year-old Jeany Marks Neely huddled with her sixteen-year-old son. "Pray, baby," were the last words Debby's daughter ever spoke.

Moments after, a morbid silence filled the air. Jeany's son, disheveled but miraculously sustaining only minor injuries, came to and located his mother in the carnage. At first he thought she was knocked unconscious as he had been. But soon he realized her injuries were far more serious. In his arms, Jeany took her final breath—succumbing to the blunt-force trauma exacted by the May 2013 Moore tornado.

I've imagined the scene as a mother's heart splintered when she received the news.

Debby Marks was still on holiday in Europe with her youngest son and his family when he knocked on her door. The red and swollen puffs around his blue eyes weren't lost on her when she let him in.

"What's wrong?" She felt her heart stop midbeat, and a chill ran frigid trails across her neck and down her arms. "Are Jess and the boys okay?" She referred to her daughter-in-law and grandchildren, mysteriously not with her son.

"They're fine."

"Then what is it?"

"Sit down, Mom."

A feverish cold settled into Debby's stomach. "I don't want to sit down."

"Please."

In numb obedience, while wrestling a growing panic, Debby fell onto a plush divan, upholstered in French flowers embroidered over a creamy background. "Just tell me."

A single ball of water formed in Levi's right eye and rolled over his reddened cheek, splashing off his quivering chin. His voice cracked when he spoke. "A tornado hit home again."

Remembering 1999, everything outside and inside Debby froze. Her limbs. Her face. Her spine. Her lungs. Her heart. Her mind. All of them paralyzed instantly. It took several seconds for any of them to release.

Anxiety marked her son's expression while he waited for her to react.

In a flood, Debby's brain released a thousand

questions simultaneously. "Is your dad all right? Loraine? Jeany? Josette? The kids?" Debby gulped air. "Is our house okay?" She thought she saw a nearly imperceptible flinch in Levi's face.

Tears began cutting a channel over his stoic features. His words came out hoarse. "Jeany. She's not with us anymore."

"Is she in the hospital?" Subconscious refusal to comprehend what she had just heard caused Debby to question.

"I'm not sure where they've taken her."

"Are the boys with her?"

"I doubt it."

"Your dad should go so she isn't afraid."

Levi picked up his mother's hand and gave it a gentle squeeze. "Did you hear what I said? She's not with us anymore."

"What does that mean?"

"I mean she's in heaven."

Reality crushed Debby's chest and clamped a hand over her mouth and nose. Instant torment burned against her cold horror.

The room started to spin. Solid surfaces seemed to move, like the intermittent waves of disbelief and sickening truth rolling through her now.

In that moment, Debby desperately wanted to crawl back into bed, allowing the strangling nightmare to pass. Even though deep down she knew it wouldn't happen. Her life would never be the same again. No matter how much she wanted it, no matter what anyone else would do or say, she could not bring her daughter back. Debby's undesired journey into the depths of grief, depression, and post-traumatic stress disorder had just begun.

As if this weren't enough, they would soon discover they had another problem—a practical dilemma making their distance from home even harder to contend with.

They were in Europe, stuck thousands of miles and an ocean away from the United States. Debby and her youngest children were separated from the rest of their grieving clan. Getting tickets home wasn't going to be easy—or fast.

The tornado had hit Moore on Monday, but it was Thursday before they could fly out of Germany—an eternity while they tried to process the inconceivable. All they could do was cluster together in prayer and disbelief while the seconds passed at an agonizing pace.

Finally, Thursday arrived. Unconscious in her motions, Debby stepped onto the German Jetway. A somber quiet followed her into the plane when she boarded. As she buckled, all she could think of was what awaited her when they touched down.

Arriving in Oklahoma, the landscape was mostly unrecognizable. Instead of familiar streets neatly lined with brick houses and well-trimmed yards, the neighborhood was devastated like a war zone.

Debby's throat tightened at the sights and smells. A mangled car leaned against the stripped-down branches of a skeletal tree. The stench of natural gas stung her nose. A tattered flag waved staunchly, the only survivor from a local business reduced to rubble. Goose pimples sprouted on her arms at the exposed root bases of huge oak trees gutted from the ground, raw earth permeating the air.

Under a collapsed roof, large handwritten red letters spelled WE R STRONG. Debby pushed a sickly taste back down her throat. She didn't want to be strong.

Well-meaning friends and neighbors streamed in and out of Debby's life over mind-numbing days. Most spoke from their heads, not understanding it was too much for Debby's heart.

"I know it hurts, but God needed Jeany more than you did."

"Jeany's in a better place."

"Jeany wouldn't want you to cry."

"She fulfilled her purpose, and it was time for her to go home."

With gentle touches, soothing voices, and the best of intentions, other stinging platitudes made Debby want to run away. She knew their motive was not to deepen the pulsating wounds vibrating in every cell of her body. So she simply smiled and nodded with each new nettle.

"You know God never gives us more than we can handle."

"This too will pass—time will heal your wounds."

"I know how you feel."

"You need to be strong for the rest of your family."

Even if one or all of these were true, in the violent moments of fresh grief, these sentiments did nothing to ease Debby's pain. As a matter of fact, they deepened her sorrow immensely. And yet she remembered times in her own past when she had stumbled over words, wondering what to say when standing in the shadows of unrequited grief. And so she smiled compassionately while she walked one fiery, determined, and brutal step at a time through the long valley where midnight seems to never end.

When Debby told me her story, the first word that came to my mind was *courageous*. This woman staunchly resolved to continue on when what she really wanted was to join her daughter in heaven. She wasn't suicidal, but there was an undeniable thinness between the wants of her body in contrast to those of her soul.

The second thing I noted was her compassion. Debby didn't blame people for trying their best to console her, even though their fumbled attempts often made her cringe. Instead, she swelled with sympathy for the well-wishers who yearned to comfort her.

As I write this, it's the one-year anniversary of Debby's loss. While people around the world have gone on with their lives, she and her family still deal with the aftereffects of the 2013 Moore tornado. This is one of the hardest aspects of dealing with trauma—the world of the griever stops, while the rest spins on. After the bereavement food is consumed and visiting mourners have returned to their own lives, people like Debby are left to deal with their post-traumatic stress, to try to make sense of senseless situations. This is especially difficult, because grief does not always unfold in orderly strides, though the stages are predictable.

Jennie Wright, RN and certified grief counselor, author of *Back to Life: Your Personal Guidebook to Grief Recovery*, shares "7 Stages of Grief: Through the Process and Back to Life" on her website, www.recover-from-grief.com/7-stages-of-grief.html.

Through her work, Wright helps those who mourn know they are not crazy or alone. Based on her intuitive understanding and practical knowledge, she tells us that when mourning any loss, we can anticipate the following stages, though they won't necessarily present themselves in this order.

> 1. *Shock and denial.* Shock temporarily shields us with emotional protection so we aren't over-whelmed all at once. We often react in numb disbelief when we get the news of a loved one's death. Denying our unwanted reality is a natural coping mechanism by which the mind attempts to avoid pain. This stage can last for minutes, hours, days, or weeks.
>
> 2. *Pain and guilt.* Unbearable pain often replaces shock as we transition from one stage to another. This part, though excruciating, is crucial to complete healing. Any attempt to escape from pain and guilt through drugs, alcohol, food, avoidance, or other measures will only prolong the pain we hope to hide from. Facing remorse for what we did or didn't do with our loved one, other guilty feelings, the chaotic and scary aspects of our situation, or anything else we

want to deny are powerful propellants to guide us through what we can't get over.

3. *Anger and bargaining.* Helpless frustration in circumstances we can't change soon gives way to anger. We may lash out and lay unwarranted blame on someone else. We may rail against fate or God. "Why?" reverberates unanswered when we bargain in vain with God to reverse what we cannot reverse.

4. *Depression, reflection, and loneliness.* Friends and family may think we should be getting on with our lives at this point, when a long period of sad reflection overtakes us. But it is a normal and necessary part of the grieving process. During this time, we finally realize the depth of our loss. Depression can spur isolation, reflection, and focus on memories of the past. Emptiness and despair smother any consideration for reinitiating former daily activities.

5. *The upward turn.* At this point, we begin to adjust to life without our beloved. Order, calmness, and glimpses of hope periodically lessen the physical symptoms, and our depression begins to lift slightly, although it's common to fall back for temporary and shorter spans while we heal.

6. *Reconstruction and working through.* Our minds start working more coherently again, and we become more functional when we

reach this point in the process. We are now capable of seeking realistic solutions to problems resulting from life without our loved one. Practical thoughts are once again possible, while reconstructing our lives (including financial rebuilding) allows us to occasionally feel normal again.

7. *Acceptance and hope.* The final stage takes us to a place where we can deal with the reality of our situation. Acceptance does not necessarily mean happiness, but it does offer us moments of peace. Periodic smiles, some even accompanied by laughter, make their return. Given the pain and turmoil we've experienced, we will never completely return to the carefree, untroubled person we were before the tragedy. But we will find a way to move forward through life—different, potentially bolder.

When we first start to look forward and actually make plans for our future, we may wrestle with a sense of shame for leaving our loved one's memory behind. This is based on false guilt. Sadness will always drape our memories of those who are no longer with us, but it's okay to remember special moments we shared. It is then we begin to anticipate good times to come and once again find joy in the experience of living.

According to experts in the field, identifying the normalcy of grieving helps sufferers fully resolve each phase while empowering them to transition to the next at the appropriate time. The danger lies in missing part of the process. Post-traumatic stress disorder lingers when we get stuck in one of the stages and repeatedly cycle over and over in unresolved grief.

Thankfully, Debby has chosen to face the necessary steps in her grief and is making strides toward finding purpose as she walks through a loss she'll never get over. Yes, she has questions. Yes, her agony at times is torturous and raw. Yes, she can express defensiveness when attack is perceived. Yes, she wrestles with God. But she has learned to take off the mask, unfettered by protocol or political correctness, and like Job, tell God how she really feels.

Debby credits a particular decision for helping her heal. Early on, she determined to lean on the strength of Jesus, no matter how bad she felt, and to unearth all the positives she could muster, even when they seemed impossible to find. Let's face it, good news doesn't always make itself obvious, especially in tragedy. So we must plan to dig deep. But as Debby discovered from a few words scrawled on yellowed fibers, the treasure makes the hunt worthwhile.

They were sifting through the wreckage when someone found a note written in Jeany's own hand. The day it was handed to Debby, she held the fragile piece of lined tablet paper with trembling fingers. It read, "One task a day. Live, love, laugh. Keep silent. Keep God close. Love the boys."

Debby clutched those words to her mother's breast. Before her death, Jeany was a nurse whose life exuded hope and healing. The swirling vortex had carried Jeany's soul from her body and deposited it in heaven. But the moment she read her daughter's words, Debby knew Jeany's impact on earth wasn't finished.

Jeany's legacy became part of Debby's mission, and today she inspires others with her daughter's heart. Debby listens to the stories of others and offers the hope she's found in Jesus. Reminding us to keep God close. To love those entrusted to us. To live and laugh as we fulfill at least one task a day. This passion gets Debby out of bed in the morning and helps her get through each moment.

A year and ten days after the Moore tornado took Jeany's life then dissipated into a clearing Oklahoma sky, Debby penned these words on her Facebook wall. A living testimony to the love of a mother, the faith of an imperfect woman, struggling to survive what most of us can't imagine, yet exuding peace many won't understand.

God bless all of you who shared our grief on Jeany's anniversary. I cannot believe it's been a year since my baby left us, swept into the arms of Jesus! I still struggle with why, yet I know why—I'm just selfish and want her here with me and her family. I miss her absence when we have our family get-togethers, her sweet smile, orneriness, intelligence, fun, etc.

I could imagine Debby fighting tears as she typed.

I miss her every moment of every day! I will never be whole again—only you who have carried a child for nine months, a wonderful miraculous being that is yours in mind and body, felt and held, will know this kind of pain.

As I read her words, I thought of my own children.

I want you to know how important salvation is—none of us has the promise of tomorrow, do we? Please think on this. Life here is fleeting, uncertain, and painful—that is why Jesus came to give us hope and eternal life. My prayer for you, dear brothers and sisters, is that you accept Jesus as your own personal Savior. This is my love message to you.

Debby speaks of confident expectation in life after death. Of once again seeing her child when she crosses the threshold from here into eternity. While on earth, Debby has endured the emotional roller coaster of loss beyond comprehension, with its unpredictable highs, lows, and setbacks. She has encountered those who mean no harm when they tell the bereaved what he or she *should* be feeling or doing. Some words have stung, while some have soothed, but Debby learned from all of them and came away with an unasked-for gift she now offers others—experiential empathy.

Experiential empathy is a depth of care, compassion, and love for a person who's hurting because you've been there and walked through that. Words are unneeded; it's now a part of who you are. Debby is reaching back to lead others through dark tunnels similar to the one she has experienced.

Ultimately, there are three ways of delivery in a valley experience. In our final pages, we'll discuss the various outcomes we might encounter from post-traumatic stress. The light of hope shines through every one, giving us hope that we can get through.

INSIDER INSIGHTS

Emotional Healing

- "Just Cry" by Mandisa is an appropriate response to the agony of losing your child. No one can mandate your boundaries for mourning. This is personal. This is unique. This is your grief. Allow the healing God placed in human tears to flow as long as you need. He understands—His Son died a torturous death.
- We've all said things that on mental review make us cringe. If someone offers a platitude, cliché, or the quick fix with a Bible verse approach, try to focus on the motive of their heart, not the failings of their tongue.
- Find a symbol(s) you can carry with you to memorialize your loved one. You need not forget—it is healthy to remember someone who cannot be replaced.

Practical Help

- Get intentional about physical exercise. It's no coincidence the first four letters of the word *health* spell *heal*. Walking outdoors, dancing to uplifting music, light weight lifting, anything that helps you break a sweat can infuse your body, mind, and soul with moments of relief. Recent studies have shown we hold trauma in our muscles, and serious exercise allows our bodies to release pent-up trauma—especially when we tremor.

- When someone says, "Let me know if I can do anything for you," have the courage to take them up on the offer. On my website, anitabrooks.com, I offer a condensed "Let Me Know List" with ideas of common things a hurting person might need. Send your friends there, or print it out to use yourself.

- Good news doesn't always make itself immediately obvious—often we must search for it, especially in tragedy. When we do, it can show up in strange places, like an offered smile, a helping hand, or as in Debby's case, a note from beyond the grave. While I was writing this book, my pastor challenged our congregation to report at least one piece of good news for thirty days. Go on the hunt and document what you find. Refer to your good news list when the pain feels unbearable.

Spiritual Comfort

- When someone dies, questions arise about suffering, but God answers our questions in Luke 16:19–31. We see a beautiful image of angels carrying Lazarus to Abraham in paradise, proving that those who accept Christ (and this can happen in the final milliseconds) are comforted and cared for when crossing from life on earth to life eternal.

- God comes alongside us in our hard times so we can comfort others (see 2 Corinthians 1:3–5). When they are troubled, we will give them the same comfort God has given us. Like the suffering of childbirth, helping others brings purpose to the pain and lessens its sting.

- When our hearts are troubled, the last thing we want to hear is someone saying, "Cheer up." As Proverbs 25:20 tells us, "Like one who takes away a garment on a cold day, or like vinegar poured on a wound, is one who sings songs to a heavy heart." Use your experiential empathy to prevent you from doing to others what doesn't feel good to you.

GUIDED PRAYER

Heavenly Father,

I can't think of a single thing to thank You for right now. But even though I don't feel like it, and sometimes I'm pretty mad at You, I'm going to praise You anyway.

So thank You for not tiring of my grief. Thank You for meeting me day or night. Thank You for listening to my confusion, my hurts, and my complaints. Thank You for not pushing me to rush past my pain. Thank You for holding on to me when I'm about to let go of You.

But most of all, thank You for truly understanding what a parent needs when their child is taken. I can't fathom what it must have been like for You to choose us over Your Son. If someone would have asked for my approval before going through this, I would have said no. Thank You for Your strength in my weakness and for doing more than I can possibly imagine.

CHAPTER 12

Valley Freedom

C an I tell you a secret?

For years I hated it when people said to me, "You just need to let go and let God."

The problem was, I desperately wanted to, but how do you let go of things you can't get over? I wrestled with shame because it sounded so simple. Apparently something was wrong with me—otherwise I would do what I wanted instead of holding on to the fears I detested. Like Paul in Romans 7:15–24, I struggled to understand myself and why I sometimes acted in opposition to what I truly desired.

Unbeknownst to me at the time, I grappled with shadows of PTSD symptoms from a series of things I'd experienced in my childhood and recent past. There were times I identified with Job where he cursed the day he was born and longed for death to carry him away from his terrors (see Job 3). Except I didn't really want to die—I just wanted the pain to go away.

But those hard times taught me good lessons. I now carry my own level of experiential empathy, a deep compassion that comes from having walked through darkness. When others hurt, I may not understand exactly what they are going through, but my gut aches for them. I care deeply. When I say I'll pray, the words aren't spoken mindlessly—I mean them. I want to reach back to the place I've come from and comfort the wounded grasping for God's healing light.

I've also come to realize things about hurting people I didn't realize before:

- No one wants to feel bad—deep down, we'd rather experience happiness than get attention.
- Letting go of what you can't control is one of the hardest things a human being will ever face.
- You don't simply pull yourself up by the bootstraps or snap yourself out of clinical depression; it's often attached to unresolved grief.
- We don't just grieve in death. Any loss—whether it's good health, peaceful relationships, dependable finances, or anything else we count as security—can throw us unprepared and fumbling into the mourning process.
- Anxiety comes from knowing you are helpless to fix or change a pain-filled experience.
- Most people have either walked through a dark valley, or are getting ready to and don't know it yet.
- If you can find a purpose, something contributing to a greater good, it will help you get out of bed in the morning and take another step toward lasting freedom from past pain.

But what if, instead of inspiring you, my last statement strikes a nerve? You might say, "I don't have the energy to help anyone else. Right now it takes every ounce of my strength just to exist."

I get it.

Sometimes the appropriate thing is simply to rest in God's arms and let Him shower you with love and acceptance while you struggle to get your bearings. Don't beat yourself up if you require medical assistance to get through your current circumstances. As Saundra Dalton-Smith, MD, says, "Some people need medicine and counseling right alongside the prayer and fasting."

I would add conversely, "Some people need prayer and fasting right alongside the medicine and counseling."

So before I go any further, if no one else tells you this, regardless of your mind-set, let me say, you are important. Your traumas matter. You are worthy of restoration. Grieving anything takes time, so give yourself permission for a temporary time-out if needed.

But equally, I want to encourage you not to give up, because you might miss out on something beautiful right around the corner. So don't stop walking too soon. Take your five-minute breather, then take another step.

Post-traumatic stress in the ordinary woman or man can originate in different ways: childhood abuse, sexual attack, identity crisis, serious money problems, unachievable expectations, loss of possessions, betrayal by a loved one, debilitation from illness or accident, the death of someone we don't know how to live without, or a myriad of other sorrows. Regardless of what or why we are traumatized, whether it's one big dramatic event or an accumulation of many things piled on top of one another, the fact is, when our souls ache, everything about our entire lives is affected.

As I've written this book, a new series of Job-type circumstances—illnesses, accidents, relationship problems, financial issues, and death—have pummeled my life. No aspect of my life was untouched by worries and wounds; the mere mass of it all threatened to send me back into the valley. But having learned from the past, I knew God was capable of miracles, even for my twenty-first-century problems.

As I wrote, the pressures built, and I began to pray. *Lord, I don't know how You're going to get me through this, but You've done it before, so I'll trust You to push the storms back and shine Your light in the darkness.* He did not fail.

One of the most difficult things I faced was a barrage of cancer diagnoses for family and friends. One after another, the calls, messages, texts, and prayer requests flooded in. But it was a special friend named Pam who was one of the hardest hits. Younger than me, diagnosed with colon cancer, she passed from life on earth to life in eternity within six months.

On March 24, Pam told us she was being moved to a hospice house. She said they weren't giving up and reminded us that God's hands aren't tied. She promised to follow up with another post the next day when she knew more. But she didn't. Pam would not post again.

On March 29, 2014, a precious woman of God left this earth, and I believe that, like Lazarus in Luke 16:19–31, she was carried into paradise. Though she fought to the end, she'd made peace with her Maker. I doubt she would come back to earth if she could.

But those who are left to mourn, including myself, have not gotten over her death—nor will we. Instead, we must process our loss through the stages of grief, even though for Pam her death is a gain, because the valley of the shadow of death never fails to lead followers of Jesus past pain into lasting freedom—one way or another.

Anytime we face a valley of trauma, there are three variations of where it might point us.

1. First, some are saved *from* walking into the valley and are allowed a last-minute detour away from its painful path.
2. Some are saved *through* the valley, where it brings us to our knees and we humble ourselves before the cross of Christ, confess our rebellion, and say yes to His loving offer to guide us through life.
3. Some, like Pam, are saved *by* the valley and ushered into paradise where our road-weary souls find permanent rest and refreshment, never again to cry or concern ourselves with traumas and trials.

Many of us will walk different but equally dark valleys. The landscape may differ, but there are crucial steps I believe we all must take if we're going to get through.

My mom first told me about the tool that got me started—a book titled *Prayer Can Change Your Life* by Dr. William R. Parker and Elaine St. Johns. What impressed me was the scientific experiment they set up to determine whether prayer truly made a difference, or whether positive effects were based on emotional persuasion in the mind.[10]

Let's face it, how many people—even among professing Christians—do we know who genuinely experience the abundant life promised in the Bible? We are like the reverend who honestly divulged, "I have been praying for many years, and there must be either more to prayer than I know about or much less than I've always hoped."

So what are we missing?

The investigators decided to test the hypothesis of four perceptions:

1. Prayer is a delusion and doesn't work at all.
2. Prayer doesn't work on principle, but by dispensation of a whimsical power which plays favorites and can be bribed. . .sometimes.
3. People don't pray.
4. People pray amiss.

What they determined was that the first three proved absolutely false and the fourth quite generally true. My experiences, interviews, and studies stand in agreement with their results. Combining my personal conclusions with their findings, I developed a twelve-step map to guide me through dark valleys in the most efficient and powerful way.

Some elements you'll recognize; some are new revelations. It's the comprehensive mixture that makes the difference.

1. *Face my inner demons and root out any painful emotions I've tried to bury.* Effective prayer addresses the specific issues of fear, false guilt, shame, and hate. I may need professional assistance and/or brutally honest friends to find the truth hidden beneath layers I've used to cover, but I must practice emotional honesty to receive benefit from my prayers.

2. *Meditate on the Bible (deep reflection in privacy and silence).* Meditation provides insights, keys, and strategies I otherwise miss. I must look beneath the surface of scriptures for answers I seek.

As I read each passage, I ask, "What is God saying to me?"

Humans are not capable of focusing on two distinctly opposite thoughts at the same time. This is where the healing balm of meditation offers its powerful medicine. I have found no other resource on earth with the restoring effects of the Bible. When my mind is focused on God's love, guidance, and wisdom, I am strengthened to take another step toward the end of my valley.

3. *Take a risk and believe God.* This is different from believing *in* God. I dare to imagine best-case scenarios.

I practice faith in trusting in what I can't yet see as it aligns with the good things God wants for me. Whether He saves me from the valley, through the valley, or by the valley, I put my hope in Him.

4. *Pray with thanksgiving as outlined in Philippians 4:6.* "Do not be anxious about anything, but in every situation, by prayer and petition, with thanksgiving, present your requests to God." I make my prayers a confident statement versus a puny question. I thank God in advance for good reports I trust are on the way.

5. *Pray last thing before falling asleep.* My subconscious does not sleep, nor does God. I invite the Holy Spirit's presence throughout the night. I let God mind my business and let love feed my subconscious as I rest at peace.

6. *Wake up knowing Jesus is waiting to talk with me.* I've trained myself to give my first awareness to God. I resolve not to dread my day. I make a fresh start by saying, "Thank You, Daddy, I'm glad You woke me up. I will rejoice in this day You have made." I also make it a point not to rush off until He has answered. Conversation is a two-way communication. Chattering at Him doesn't work—I can't learn if I don't listen.

7. *Set daily goals.* These may include: Get up. Get dressed. Show up for life. Write my gratitude list.

8. *Pray for others, including and especially world leaders.* So often we get sucked into believing we can do nothing about global economies, wars and rumors of wars, political upheavals, or crises in our own front yards, but this is not true. We can make a difference.

One prayer at a time, we can tap into a power far greater than anything we can imagine. I ask myself, "What might you accomplish if you pray in faith?"

9. *Pray in words and actions for my enemies.* This is a tough one. But I know from experience the blessing I receive when I do this, whether privately and anonymously (for me this has proven most effective) or openly. Proverbs 25:21–22 and Romans 12:19–21 both outline the benefits of doing what goes against our instincts.

10. *Determine to affect at least one person or situation daily in a positive way.* I open my eyes for awareness of someone else's needs. I strive to live love-centered rather than self-centered. To give rather than take. Become a good news reporter in a world saturated with bad publicity.

11. *Say yes to at least one thing daily and no to at least one thing daily.* Most of us are harried, too busy, and overwhelmed. This leads to an accumulation of stresses, burnout, adrenal overload, and even mild forms of PTSD. I give myself permission to do at least one thing aligned with my talents, gifts, and deepest desires every day—while I decline those things I'm not made to tackle. I've realized an empty cup has nothing to offer a thirsty person. If you give a sip to everyone who asks, there's nothing left to quench a real need.

12. *Concentrate on seeing myself as the person Jesus sees in me.* This is not the person others perceive or who I've seen in my past self. This is the potential God endowed in me, the person He created me to be. I am not an

accident or a cosmic glitch. I am created on purpose with purpose to fulfill a purpose.

My job while on earth, no matter how many breaths I have left, is to figure out who I am and what I'm supposed to do—then act on the voice of truth, not echoes of lies. I dare to face every day. I determine to walk through challenges with tenacity. I resolve to partner with God in transforming problems into miracles. I choose to see my valley as an adventure with Christ as my guide.

As we near the end of our journey together, I hope you are encouraged. I cannot promise your own path will come easy. If you deal with post-traumatic stress, anything can trigger a flashback of your difficult event. Hated reminders can haunt you. A particular restaurant, a specific model and color of a vehicle, a name, a food, a song, a sound, or a smell can take you back to a place you long to avoid. Unhappy anniversary dates will remind you of something you wish to forget. But you have a choice in how you react.

Don't crumble, don't cave, don't cower. Walk.

I especially like something Cecil Murphey, author of *90 Minutes in Heaven* and *Knowing God, Knowing Myself*, said. In the latter book, Cecil shares an ongoing prayer: "God, heal the parts of me that don't want to be healed."[11]

I've found healing in the Bible for the parts of me that don't want to be healed. Reading God's Word moves me past the pain into lasting freedom. It's why I smile and laugh today. Jesus is my strength and confidence. He offers you the same good news.

Today, while there's breath in your body, you have time to ask yourself these questions.

Have I really lived?

Have I made efforts to pursue the dreams God placed in my heart?

Have I acted in love?

Have I made a difference?

Be careful how you answer.

We get stuck when we set overly high expectations of ourselves; they become unachievable. For instance, when you consider if you've really lived, don't browbeat yourself if you haven't chased daring and adventure. The woman or man quietly conversing with God on the behalf of others has lived a courageous life.

Have you pursued the dreams God placed in your heart? If there's something you always wanted to do but were afraid to try, take one action toward making it reality today. If you don't have the strength or ability to do so directly, then find a way to do it vicariously. Go there in your imagination, find a book, video, or audio recording of someone who has achieved this dream, and travel with them as they describe it.

Whether or not you've acted in love in the past, you can now. Are there bridges you should mend? Relationships with unfinished business? Unresolved grief your soul thirsts to express? Take courage and communicate your love now while you still can.

Have you made a difference? The ways we can do this are many. Not everyone is called to stand in a spotlight, on a stage, or in an arena. I think of the thousands who helped Nehemiah rebuild the Jerusalem wall, most unidentified, and yet to complete the project their work was necessary.

Your smile given to a stranger, eye contact with someone serving you, an anonymous gift provided to someone in need, a card sent by mail, a listening ear offered without advice or fix-its, telling someone what they did right instead of what they did wrong, speaking someone's name, a prayer lifted in your private space. These small gratuities can change someone else's life. You can be their difference.

When the next tragedy strikes, when the next struggle hits, steel yourself to say, "God, I look forward to seeing how You're going to get me through this." Then watch Him heal your heart, mind, and soul while using your trial to show you meaning as you help others.

Because of the things I've been through, I now understand the haunting beauty of wilderness walks, unwanted journeys on lonely paths where well-meaning people tell you what you need to do. Try as they might, they don't comprehend the depth of your pain or your desire to be anywhere else but where you are.

However, though wilderness walks feel dry and desolate or deep and dark, they offer an oasis in the desert of life, for they allow God to get us all to Himself where He speaks to us intimately through quiet time with Him. It is here we see that God—no one or nothing else—is our Provider.

Sometimes God needs to separate us from every-thing and everyone so we will finally see and hear how much He loves and cares about our every need.

I can now say that I thank Him for each traumatic event I've lived through. Miracles have occurred because of the troubles I've seen. From these experiences, I've realized three things.

There are absolutely life-changing things we never get over, but we can get through.

God does not abandon us, even when it feels like He has.

People and hardships haven't changed since Job walked the earth, and we can take courage from knowing we are not the first to suffer.

Life is full of mountains and valleys. Whether you walk them in dry and arid deserts or beneath the waves on deep ocean beds, hold on to Auschwitz survivor Edie Eger's words: "The Twenty-Third Psalm says, 'Though I walk through the valley of the shadow of death.' It does not say, 'Slow down.' It does not say, 'Stop.' It does not say, 'Pitch a tent.' It does not say, 'Build a house.' It says, 'Walk.' "

Sometimes a tiny step in the right direction starts you on the one trail that will make the biggest difference in your life. You are made to be God's holy dwelling; you are a living miracle—let that define you and propel you into the light you were made to bask in.

If you don't believe you have the strength to take one more step, then believe God. Get back up when you get knocked down. You can't see the good things He has in store for you from the ground. You can't experience the great things embedded in your future if you don't step into it.

Whether you are delivered from the valley, through the valley, or by the valley, the presence of Jesus can shine into your gloom. No matter how you feel today, the darkness cannot prevail forever; even death cannot hide from the power of God's healing. This is our promise, our hope, our truth. You need never walk alone again—with God you will get through.

INSIDER INSIGHTS

Emotional Healing

- "Long Way Home" by Steven Curtis Chapman takes us on a musical voyage, aptly describing how wearying a life of trauma can feel while inspiring us with hope for the final outcome. Just don't give up too early, because you're not home yet—you're still alive for a reason.

- Expect rather than berate yourself for extreme emotions and behaviors. Review the stages of grief, and give yourself permission to experience each one. It's common to circle back and forth, so don't admonish yourself for revisiting places you've already been. Anger is part of this process, so try to find a safe person you can vent to and get the gunk out.

- Prepare to forgive. First, yourself. For anything you regret, confess it, turn away from doing anything like it again, ask God to forgive you, then accept His willingness to throw it into the sea of forgetfulness. Second, forgive those who will deepen your hurt with well-intentioned but not-so-helpful comments. Remember, grief belongs to the griever, so don't let thoughtless or ill-timed words take your focus off what you need to do in your unique situation.

Practical Help

- None of us knows whether we have another minute, hour, year, or decade. Before time runs out, brainstorm a list of every happy memory you can recall. Then go to each person who was a part of it and say thank you. Make phone calls, send letters or cards, email, post messages on social media—whatever form you can find to show them your genuine gratitude.

- Accept specific, offered assistance. Don't steal God's blessings from those who want to do acts of kindness. If they want to clean, let them clean. If they want to run errands for you, let them run errands. If they want to bring you a meal, let them bring it.

- Do what you can when you can. Every day, try to think of at least one reason why you might exist, and if at all possible, take action toward fulfilling that purpose.

Spiritual Comfort

- When fear or the past paralyzes you, meditate on this passage: "I am able to do all things through Him who strengthens me"

(Philippians 4:13 HCSB). Focus on the word *I* first. Out loud say, "*I* am able to do all things through Him who strengthens me," three times. Next, "I *am* able to do all things through Him who strengthens me," three times. Then, "I am *able* to do all things through Him who strengthens me," three times. Continue in this pattern until you have focused on each individual word in the entire passage.

- Take a fresh step with fresh faith. Even in your deepest pain, you never walk alone. God walks with you through every difficulty (see John 16:33).

- Resist giving in to your post-traumatic stressors and the ploys of the evil one, trusting our God of grace will restore you Himself, making you strong, firm, and steadfast until you come through your dark valley and step into new light (see 1 Peter 5:8–10).

GUIDED PRAYER

Dear Jesus,

When I am in the throes of something I will never get over, I need to know You are with me every step of the way. Thank You for understanding my rattled emotions. Thank You for loving me when I feel my most unlovable. And thank You that one day, even though I can't imagine it now, You will lead me into a place of healing light. For now, I will exercise faith in spite of what I feel. One day I will look back on my life and see my footprints embedded within Your own because, before I took one step, You walked the valley before me. I hide my hope in You—no matter what comes next.

ENDNOTES

1. "Post-Traumatic Stress Disorder: The Symptoms," Dr. Phil, November 14, 2002, https://www.drphil.com/advice/post-traumatic-stress-disorder-the-symptoms/.

2. US Census Bureau, America's Families and Living Arrangements: 2010, "Living Arrangements of Children under 18 Years/1 and Marital Status of Parents by Age, Sex, Race, and Hispanic Origin/2 and Selected Characteristics of the Child for all Children 2010," http://www.census.gov/population/www/socdemo/hh-fam/cps2010.html.

3. Mona Chalabi, "Dads That Don't Live with Their Children: How Many Stay in Touch?," *Guardian*, November 19, 2013, https://www.theguardian.com/news/datablog/2013/nov/20/non-resident-dads-relationship-children.

4. Scott D. Pierce, "LDS TV Host Turns Family Searches into His Life's Work," Deseret News, September 1, 2008, https://www.deseretnews.com/article/705381359/LDS-TV-host-turns-family-searches-into-his-lifes-work.html.

5. Scott Pelley (correspondent), *60 Minutes*, season 46, episode 9, "The War Within: Treating PTSD," aired November 24, 2013 on CBS, transcript at https://www.cbsnews.com/news/the-war-within-treating-ptsd/.

6. Les Christie, "10 Hottest Housing Markets for 2014," CNN, January 23, 2014, https://money.cnn.com/gallery/real_estate/2014/01/23/hottest-housing-markets/index.html.

7. Marty Gervais, "Sage Advice on How to Avoid the Family Fight," originally published in the Windsor Star, The Family War, https://thefamilywar.com/media_tfw/windsorstar_061110.html, accessed December 28, 2018.

8. Rob Moll, "The New Workplace Romance," Focus on the Family, 2003, https://www.focusonthefamily.com/marriage/sex-and-intimacy/managing-temptation/the-new-workplace-romance, accessed December 28, 2018.

9. Pelley, *60 Minutes*, "The War Within: Treating PTSD."

10. William R. Parker and Elaine St. Johns, *Prayer Can Change Your Life* (New Jersey: Prentice Hall Press, 1957).

11. Cecil Murphey, *Knowing God, Knowing Myself* (New York: Revell, 2011), 17–18.

ABOUT THE AUTHOR

Anita Agers-Brooks inspires others to overcome and thrive, by telling her own dramatic stories, and sharing those of people who also believe, "It's never too late for a fresh start with fresh faith." Anita is a speaker on circuit for Stonecroft Ministries, www.stonecroft.org, a popular keynote and session guest for various national, state, and regional association conferences, as well as a leadership/staff trainer for organizations around the country. She also speaks to churches and Christian colleges, as well as public school systems.

WHEN YOU NEED SUPPORT, LET GOD HELP. . .

God Is in the Small Stuff 20th Anniversary Edition

Bruce & Stan's bestselling *God Is in the Small Stuff* is back and better than ever in this special 20th-anniversary edition! And their message for you is as timely today as it was two decades ago. While encouraging you not to disregard the minor, insignificant things in life, *God Is in the Small Stuff* invites a better understanding of God's infinite character, reminding you that He is a personal and intimate God, involved in every detail of your life.
Paperback / 978-1-64352-070-4 / $7.99

Letting Go and Trusting God

Letting Go and Trusting God is a devotional that looks at both the well-thought-out choices and impulse decisions of biblical people. These devotions can gently help readers understand how to make wise decisions, no matter what life throws their way.
Paperback / 978-1-63409-210-4 / $5.99